INDEX
ON CENSORSHIP

INDEX ON CENSORSHIP 6 2000

WEBSITE NEWS UPDATED WEEKLY

www.indexoncensorship.org
contact@indexoncensorship.org
tel: 020 7278 2313
fax: 020 7278 1878

Volume 29 No 6 November/December 2000 Issue 197

Index on Censorship (ISSN 0306-4220) is published bi-monthly by a non-profit-making company: Writers & Scholars International Ltd, Lancaster House, 33 Islington High Street, London N1 9LH. *Index on Censorship* is associated with Writers & Scholars Educational Trust, registered charity number 325003 *Periodicals postage*: (US subscribers only) paid at Newark, New Jersey. Postmaster: send US address changes to *Index on Censorship* c/o Mercury Airfreight International Ltd Inc., 365 Blair Road, Avenel, NJ 07001, USA
© This selection Writers & Scholars International Ltd, London 1999
© Contributors to this issue, except where otherwise indicated

Subscriptions (6 issues per annum)
Individuals: Britain £39, US $52, rest of world £45
Institutions: Britain £44, US $80, rest of world £50
Speak to Tony Callaghan on 020 7278 2313
or email tony@indexoncensorship.org

Cover: *It's a child's world – after we've finished with it*
Original artwork by Ralph Steadman

Index has made every effort to discover copyright owners of material in this issue. Any errors or omissions are inadvertent.

EDITORIAL

Comedy of terrors

Free speech is back in fashion: censorship could be on the run. After years of crying in the wilderness, it seems people generally are engaged in the issue as never before. The incorporation of the European Convention on Human Rights into UK law as of 2 October, has, for the first time in domestic law, given us a benchmark against which to measure the length and breadth of our free expression – the foundation, we at *Index* believe, of all other rights. Given the nature of British law, it will take time for the cases to be tried and the precedents established; but despite the cynical denigration of a few, we should all be better off when hit with libel suits, the Obscene Publications Act, a D-notice or the like. And that is what *Index* has been quietly working to achieve for almost 30 years.

Not that we are omniscient. We don't think there's much that escapes our notice on the censorship front but, as with our banned music issue a couple of years ago, our foray into comedy has been a revelation.

Like music, comedy really can reach the parts other, more arcane forms cannot: it deflates dictators, defies tyrants and, like Lear's Fool, speaks out where others prefer to hold their peace. Comedians are often the only voice for the silenced and oppressed. Whether it's Lenny Bruce getting on the tits of a US president or Bill Hicks haranguing CBS from beyond the grave, comedians get under the corporate skin and call the bluff of politicians.

Or did. There's a tendency in the West for the one-time 'alternative' comics, beloved of the young and the radical, to sell out to the networks: cash and the seductions of power have, by and large, robbed comedy of its cutting edge. The jester has gone; and we're all courtiers in soft-centred comedy love-ins and red-nose telethons that relieve only the tedium of late-night TV.

But elsewhere, comics and cartoonists are still the people who articulate ideas too dangerous for words. And there's always a price. For Iranian cartoonists and satirists reflecting on the sad state of their media today, it can be imprisonment (p153). Algeria's foremost stand-up comic Fellag, an expert on Algeria's deep-sea politics, has been forced into exile. The routines that delighted his countrymen are now performed in Parisian halls and distributed back home 'under the counter'. Comedy is no laughing matter: banning, exile, imprisonment and sudden death in dark streets make sure of that (p118). ❑

contents

O TEMPORA!
O MORONS!

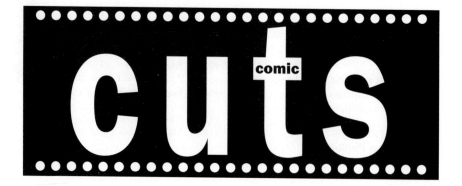

comic cuts

● **Thai cheek** In January 1997, the Professional Comedians Association of Thailand introduced strict regulations to control the content of its members' routines. Explaining that it wished to put an end to 'impoliteness on stage', the association stated that it would no longer tolerate 'obscene language', 'physical humour in which pain is implied' and, strangely, 'disrespect to a fellow comedian's parents'. What on earth had they been saying?

● **Wronged rights** Comedian Jackie Mason filed a US$25m lawsuit against five Broadway theatre groups in 1994 for their failure to nominate him in any category for a Tony Award for theatre. Mason, whose show *Politically Incorrect* received critical acclaim, complained the judges had 'abridged' his 'rights as a human being' by overlooking his claim to an award.

● **Bowdlerised sister** While on the topic of abridgement, it appears that Dr Thomas Bowdler, patriarch of the school of censorship that stripped *Gulliver's Travels*, the Old Testament and Shakespeare of their sex and thunder, was not quite the paragon that history pretends. It was actually his unremembered sister who dispatched the family name to its date with the dictionary by snipping the spicier bits of the Bard for the 1818 *Family Shakespeare*. They couldn't say so on the cover because, obviously, a woman wouldn't have known such words.

● **Twøddle** Comedian Jacob Haugaard became the first independent ever to win a seat in the Danish parliament when he was elected MP for Aarhus in September 1994. Haugaard promised electors good weather, better Christmas presents and tailwinds for cyclists. To win over the marginals, he threw in the pledge of standard-size bags for vacuum cleaners, and the right for all people to be 'dumb, ugly and rich'. Upon learning of his victory, an astonished Haugaard said: 'It's incredible that I got elected on this twøddle.'

● **By Royal Appointment: jail** The late Turkish comedian Aziz Nesin – whose surname means 'what are you?' – devoted his life to ruthlessly lampooning the establishment. His satirical newspaper *Marko Pasha* was banned repeatedly, reinventing itself under variations of the same title, including *Deceased Pasha*. In 1949, after an article against monarchy, he was simultaneously sued by King Farouk of Egypt, Shah Rezi Pehlevi and – so he claimed – Queen Elizabeth The Queen Mother for defamation, and was jailed for six months. He overcame a subsequent ban on his work by writing under a series of pen-names. His female identity, Oya Etes, was listed in the National Bibliography of Turkish Women Writers and 'her' stories became set reading in primary schools.

● **Trouble brewing** In May 1996, an Istanbul court convicted Güzel, a cartoonist with the Kurdish daily *Özgür Ülke*, of 'insulting' the republic and sentenced him to ten months in prison. Grounds for the conviction was a cartoon in a December 1994 edition which depicts a group of men in a café complaining that some customers are being served tip-top smuggled tea, while others are drinking 'inferior Turkish Republic tea'. One patron complains that the police are being served even higher-quality tea. Güzel was in the middle of a 40-month term for other, similarly offensive cartoons when sentenced.

● **Target practice** Christoph Grissemann and Dirk Stermann, Austria's most popular comedy duo, faced criminal charges in February 2000 for recommending that far-right populist Jörg Haider be 'shot' in an interview with the arts magazine *Rödr@nner*. The comments were made in October 1999 and picked up by the regional newspaper *Neues Volkblatt*, which is affiliated to the conservative People's Party. Meanwhile, youth culture is hitting back against the new coalition with a modified version of the computer game *Castle Wolfstein*. In the original, players move down corridors and shoot pictures of Hitler and Nazi soldiers. In the doctored version, the Nazis are replaced by Haider and his crönies.

● **Holy writ** The Latin Patriarchate in Jerusalem in February demanded a public apology from the producers of a 'candid camera' TV programme for an irreverent segment filmed in Italy. A hidden camera filmed an Israeli comedian, dressed as a priest, cavorting in a plaza with a 'nun', as he asked passers-by what he should do to win her heart. The 'priest' also made the sign of the cross and slapped people on the forehead as he 'blessed' them in the square. 'This offended thousands of Christians and even non-Christians in the Holy Land, and many are continuing to contact us to express their rage,' said Wadie Abu Nasser, an advisor to the Latin Patriarch of Jerusalem.

● **Non-exhaustive** A web design company in London bit off more than it could swallow when it invited its .com copywriters to submit topical jokes to a network pool. Back came the following memo from Ms Whiplash. '1. Although you may not be offended by the "jokes", there is always someone who will be, because jokes are generally about other people and their misfortunes, or their sex, gender, disability, misfortune, race, colour, creed or religion (this list is non-exhaustive). Perhaps next time that may be you. 2. As a Company we are responsible for ANY information transmitted in any format and we are obligated by law to prevent, as far as is possible and reasonable, anything that could be deemed offensive or insulting, either directly or indirectly.'

● **Victims of comedy** Two black waitresses in the UK took their employers to an industrial tribunal in September 1996 for failing to shield them from racist comedian Bernard Manning's wit. Freda Burton and Sonia Rhule told the Commission for Racial Equality how they were serving guests at the Pennine Hotel in Derby when Manning, booked as an after-dinner speaker, began his usual routine. Manning unleashed a barrage of jokes, which exposed the two waitresses to racial and sexual abuse. 'Nobody came to help us,' testified Rhule, 'and nobody stopped it.' Hotel executives, parrying their claims, declared that they had been caught in a 'Catch 22 dilemma'. An hotel spokesman said that the alternative would have been to employ white waitresses only to serve at the event, an act that would have made them liable to prosecution for racial discrimination.

● **Comedy bypass** In March 1996, four Canadian comedians were sued by Multimedia Entertainment Corporation, the makers of the *Jerry Springer* show, after they masqueraded as a sex quartet to get on to the show. With two of them posing as a married couple, another as their babysitter and the fourth as her boyfriend, the satirists wangled their way on to an episode that saw women confronting their husbands over affairs with their childminders. An unamused executive from Multimedia declared that such hoaxes 'threatened the integrity' of the show.

● **Joker juiced** A feud between NBC executive Don Ohlmeyer and presenter-turned-humorist Norm Macdonald spilled on to the airwaves in June 1997 when Ohlmeyer issued a ban on mentioning Macdonald's new comedy, *Dirty Work*. Ohlmeyer also told producers to pull all advertising for the film. Macdonald had enraged Ohlmeyer by writing a number of scripts which mocked his close friend, OJ Simpson. The action was justified in a terse statement explaining that NBC, which had until recently employed Macdonald as anchor for its *Saturday Night Live* show, did not want to 'sell a movie for a comedian it feels besmirches the network's name'.

FABIO CASTILLO

The go-between

The humorist Jaime Garzón was murdered for the only thing he took seriously: working for peace in Colombia

Jaime Garzón was shot dead in Bogotá, on his way to work at Radionet radio station, on 13 August 1999 by two individuals riding a motorbike (*Index* 3/1999, 1/2000). His satirical portrayal of public figures, and probing interviews that touched areas others dare not, made him a favourite with listeners. The public outcry at what the media dubbed the 'murder of a smile' prompted all three of the country's security agencies to become involved in the homicide investigation.

What they have unearthed so far is that the sharp-tongued satirist was murdered by one of Medellín's infamous *sicario* gangs, which make a living out of contract killings. The man suspected of hiring the gang's services is Carlos Castaño, chief of the right-wing paramilitary squads which operate under the banner of the United Self-Defence Forces of Colombia (AUC).

One can trace the events that led to Garzón's death back to 22 August 1998, when the largest left-wing guerrilla group, the Revolutionary Armed Forces of Colombia (FARC), carried out one of its mass kidnappings. From being a sideline commentator, Garzón was thrust into the centre of events after relatives of the kidnapped begged him to act as a go-between in negotiations with the FARC commander. His intervention proved successful, securing the safe release of all the hostages.

From that moment on, Garzón's help was sought by the families of all those held hostage by the FARC. Attending to them was no easy task. There are officially around 3,000 kidnappings a year, but almost as many more go unreported. Before too long, Garzón was contracted by the governor of Colombia's eastern province in October 1998 to try to establish a dialogue with local guerrillas. Documents found in the office of the country's anti-kidnapping tsar show that the authorities subsequently used Garzón as an intermediary in some 30 cases in the year leading up to his death.

The investigation into Garzón's death was assigned to public prosecutor Eduardo Meza, responsible for prosecuting crimes against journalists, of which Colombia has the highest incidence in the world. The office is currently investigating 24 murders, two cases of death threats and the brutal kidnapping of journalist Yineth Bedoya (*Index* 4/2000).

At first, the investigation seemed to stray into the surrealism that Garzón had so adroitly used in his comedy. One witness accused a former US president of masterminding the crime in an attempt to silence Garzón for 'discovering' that the Americans had run the international drug trade in collusion with the governments of Britain, Spain and the Netherlands. Others claimed to

Jaime Garzón, drawn in the year he was murdered.
Credit: Hector Ozuna

have heard death threats against Garzón from a senator who had been at the receiving end of his sharp humour. Some alluded to a crime of passion. Of the 13 hypotheses that came to light, only one lead seemed worth pursuing: the eyewitness account of a woman who was able to describe in detail the features of one of the motorbike riders who shot Garzón. A photofit picture based on her testimony was distributed throughout Colombia.

Meanwhile, the Medellín office of Colombia's secret police, the DAS, received a call from an informer pointing the finger at two hired assassins from a *sicario* gang in the neighbourhood of La Terraza. The caller said that, at the time of Garzón's murder, the two men had been away in the highlands and came back 'loaded with money'. Only one of the *sicarios* had a telephone, and his calls were tapped for 60 days. Although he made no reference to Garzón's killing during the period, he did mention committing a murder.

The suspect was arrested in October last year and, in an identity parade, was instantly recognised by the woman who had witnessed Garzón's murder. He was identified as Juan Pablo Ortiz Agudelo, better known as *El Bochas* (Mr Bowls).

News of this prompted Senator Piedad Córdoba to visit Meza at the attorney general's office. Córdoba had been kidnapped a few weeks before Garzón's murder by paramilitary leader Carlos Castaño. She claimed that, during her captivity, Castaño had made repeated references to Garzón as a 'guerrilla sympathiser'. Police investigators now began to put the pieces of the puzzle together. Looking at past press interviews with Castaño, it became apparent that he had an intense dislike of those prepared to negotiate with guerrillas. On 20 May this year, the paramilitary leader was charged with masterminding the humorist's killing and an order was issued for his arrest. He is, needless to say, still at large.

Two weeks later, the head of the La Terraza gang linked to Garzón's killing, Elkin Sánchez Mena, was himself murdered. Police found out that another gang member, Efraín Fernando González Jaramillo, had been murdered a month after Garzón's death. González turned out to be the brother of the main suspect in the 1998 murder of Elsa Alvarado and Mario Calderón, two researchers with the progressive NGO, Centro de Investigación y Educacíon Popular.

On 6 October, paramilitary commander Luis Eduardo Cifuentes Galindo, known as *El Aguila* (The Eagle), was reportedly murdered in Carcel Modelo de Bogotá prison, though it later emerged he had escaped and was in hiding. This same commander had been asked by Garzón, three days before his death, to arrange a meeting with Castaño. According to several sources, Garzón had planned to meet Castaño on 14 August, the day after he was murdered. The deaths of Sánchez and González and the disappearence of *El Aguila* are all seen as attempts by Castaño to sever any connection to Garzón's murder.

When *El Bochas* was arrested last October, a pistol was found in his possession with an accompanying letter of safe conduct. Safe conducts are issued by IV Brigade of the Colombian army in Medellín to people whose lives are under serious threat and need to carry a gun for self-defence. Garzón might have enjoyed that irony. ❏

Fabio Castillo is co-director and editor of Bogotá's Revista Alternativa.
Translated by William Escofet

ADAM PHILLIPS

The joy of sex and laughter

A psychoanalyst talks about the ambivalence and ambiguity that lie beneath the surface of what makes us laugh

URSULA OWEN *What are jokes and why do we like them?*

ADAM PHILLIPS Jokes are a way of smuggling unacceptable thoughts, feelings and ideas into a socially acceptable form. They're also ways of getting pleasure from unacceptable ideas and beliefs. I think the reason Freud was interested in jokes, and linked them with dreams and symptoms, was because jokes revealed two things: one, that we are divided against ourselves; two, that our internal divisions give us pleasure. So with jokes, as with sex, we are likely to find our preferences don't always accord with our standards. I might, for example, be very anti-racist, but find myself, nevertheless, amused by a racist joke. For Freud, this is very revealing: in a conventional sense, what a hypocrite I am. But he also says there's a great deal of internal conflict in every judgement: in a sense, I'm a racist and non-racist at the same time. Since this is difficult to manage, jokes are our contraband, our rather ingenious ways of getting pleasure from things we find unacceptable.

UO *Why is it that we love comedians so much? Why do we admire people who can laugh at other people and themselves? What do they do for us?*

AP To be amused is a fantasy of freedom: as though when one is laughing, one is released, set free from something. Again, in a way, similar to sexuality. That's very powerful.

BOZO THERAPY

Copyright (C) Gregory Christ

Don't you feel better now you're in touch
with your "inner imbecile"?

Humour, implicitly, also brings multiple points of view into the arena. One reason we find irony, for example, amusing and reassuring might be that it means there are at least two points of view about something. This is complicated: you might think jokes are exclusively about prejudice, yet I think jokes reveal that we are both immensely reassured by our prejudices – we are all anti-Semites so we can get together and make jokes about Jews – and, at the same time, are made intensely uneasy about our prejudices. Freud has this great phrase 'the laughter of unease'. There's a great deal of laughter of unease: we don't know why we're laughing, yet it's in our body. You could end up thinking people are what makes them laugh.

It's a double-edged thing: on the one hand, groups are clearly formed around jokes – jokes are social, people feel an affinity with those with whom they share a sense of humour. But jokes are also collusive – they leave people out – either you get the joke or you don't. If you don't, then you're outside. In that sense, they are very tribal or territorial. You can see why, for instance, political regimes would seek to be sustained by a currency of shared jokes, but also why they would be frightened by rival counter-cultures that shared different jokes.

UO   *There are jokes that diminish authoritarian and totalitarian regimes by making them comic or absurd. Is that also about prejudice?*

AP   It's as though there are certain people and certain regimes that depend on the illusion of consistency. What the joke reveals is inconsistency. The joke is all the time exposing points of vulnerability,

where the personality or the regime cannot sustain itself, and that is where the danger is. Anything in a regime that you can laugh at is likely to be a point of contention: wherever there's laughter, there's the debate that's being suppressed, the conflict that can't be opened up. A joke is like a diagnosis. Wherever in the system you can be amused, you've touched on something that cannot be discussed.

UO   *One of the classic ways in which, for example, East Europeans dealt with monolithic communist regimes, or the way Egyptians make jokes against themselves, is by the use of irony. How does that relate to what you're saying?*

AP   The ironist has a fantasy of internal superiority. Anyone who feels oppressed is going to need to find a position in themselves from which they don't feel oppressed. There's a certain kind of knowingness in irony, as though one has seen through something, or has a created a fiction with which to counter the thing or the regime. In that sense it's very important, because it frees people to be able to think about the things that oppress them. When you live in an oppressive system, by definition the system works to stop you having certain thoughts. Once you are able to be in an ironic position, it is as though you have found another place from which you can think about something.

A regime might create a counter-culture of certain types of irony or jokes, and these are as much integral to the regime, even though unconsciously, as the manifest dogma of ideology. There is always going to be something very nasty, very sadomasochistic, going on in the relationship between the regime and the people who are free enough to mock it.

UO   *Are you saying humour is socially constructed, or biological, or both?*

AP   I don't exactly know. People do say there are dogs that laugh. It is very easy to imagine people who aren't amused, but it is not easy to imagine a good life without amusement in it. The thing about a joke is that nobody can tell you that you aren't amused by it; they can only tell you that you shouldn't be. This tells us something interesting about authority. I might find myself immensely impressed by some authoritative figure, but still amused in some way, or mocking them, and I might feel this is involuntary. A better description of it isn't that it is involuntary, but that I need to believe that it is involuntary in order to legitimate it. I've got to think it isn't really me who's amused but something in me, something more powerful than little me. In fact, it's another bit of little me that can't take whatever it's being told. I would have thought that must be very powerful culturally; it's very interesting in Eastern European poetry. It is all something to do with a relationship with censorship, with what you can do with what you're not permitted to say or to think. That then becomes an aesthetic project: how can I disguise this so that it is both acceptable and critical?

MAYBE ONE OF THE REASONS YOUR FRIENDS TREAT YOU WITH SUCH DISRESPECT IS THE FACT YOU'VE NEVER CHANGED YOUR SHIRT...

ATLANTIC FEATURE © 1996 MARK PARISI
www.offthemark.com

ADAM PHILLIPS

UO   *Is there such a thing as a humourless person, a person who doesn't get jokes, and who is, therefore, seeing the world in some different way?*

AP   You'd have thought the humourless person like the humourless regime would be one that cannot risk a whole array of points of view around it. It is about risk and it is about coerced narrow-mindedness, to protect themselves from certain kinds of anxiety. If I demand of you that you take me utterly seriously, that you take me on my own terms, I am trying to stop you thinking certain things about me. These, presumably, are the things that I am also trying to stop me thinking about me. An awful lot of work goes into stopping people having certain thoughts about things – you need loads of policemen and lots of fear and intimidation. It's a 24-hour-a-day job.

UO   *Is the reason we admire people like Lenny Bruce that they are taking bigger risks? That they are, so to speak, cleansing themselves of their own repressions?*

AP   This is a complicated issue. There is a fantasy that the funnier a person is, the freer he is. I don't think this is entirely true. The comic is an interesting figure, somebody who flirts with the possibility of not being amusing. There is always the possibility of being ridiculed, and there is nothing more excruciating than a failed joke. So it seems to me that one of the reasons we admire comics is because they take a massive risk: they are flirting with the possibility of their own shame or humiliation. This is really dire, life-and-death stuff. We want to watch other people doing it, but we don't want to do it ourselves. Once you are being funny, you are taking a very big risk with yourself and with your audience because you set yourself up as a kind of scapegoat-hero figure.

UO   *You've talked about authoritarian regimes and the way humour might deal with them. Why is humour subversive? Does it affect these regimes? Are they not immune to the absurd by their very lack of humour?*

AP   I would have thought so. Humourlessness is a defence. But I think humour is the last thing before violence. I think there's something good about the wish to change things through persuasion, of which humour is a kind. There's a great fear about what happens when the humour breaks down, because once humour breaks down, you have nothing left. It would be optimistic to say that all you've got to do is laugh and the regime comes tumbling down, but it would be equally naive to assume that humour has no power. Once people begin to see the absurd side of things, things feel less terrifying. It is almost like psychic alchemy. There's this terrifying person or regime, and you have to find ways of looking at them or describing them so that you can do more with them. If you can be amused, or render them absurd or surreal in some way, it is as though you've then got more imaginative space inside you to look at them. I think that is what people are looking for.

UO *I can't remember descriptions of humour in the Nazi camps or in Japanese prisoner-of-war camps. Are there are certain situations when humour runs out?*

AP It would be very interesting to know what the situations are that render humour impossible. I remember being very struck once when I saw a West Indian boy of 15 who had been referred for some kind of violence. He asked me how I felt about racist jokes, so I asked him to give an example. He started to tell me a concentration camp joke. I said I didn't want him to tell me this joke, and then there was a silence. Then he said: 'I'm really glad you said that,' and I asked why. He said: 'If I'd told the joke, it would have been as though you agreed I could make a fool of you.' Until that moment, I would have thought I wanted to live in a world in which there were no sacred cows, in which nothing was beyond humour. But in that moment, I could also see how there can be a kind of spurious permissiveness in agreeing that everything is funny. There is a complicity in it.

It's like something Sartre says in his book on Baudelaire. He says there are two types of people: rebels and revolutionaries. Rebels want to keep the world exactly as it is so that they can go on rebelling against it; revolutionaries change the world. Lots of types of humour may actually be rebellious under the guise of being revolutionary. In a way, you need to sustain the regime so that you can go on laughing at it, but actually nothing changes. There might be a difference between revolutionary humour and rebellious humour.

UO   *Can jokes cross cultures? Are there any universal jokes?*

AP   There seem to be genres of jokes, and jokes seem to be about
vulnerability. But vulnerability is obviously our word, and we can't
transpose that. But it does seem, broadly speaking, that jokes are about
vulnerability and authority. My guess would be that this probably is
transcultural. What is interesting is that there are genres of jokes that
are translatable, like light bulb jokes, in which you could be a Pole or a
woman. I would also imagine that in terms of people feeling that they've
made some link or connection with people from other cultures, being
amused, or amusing them, would be a powerful way. Somebody could
feel very alien to you, but the points of shared amusement would feel
like points of affinity.

UO   *Did humour play a different role when our society was religious rather
than secular?*

AP   I think the two regulated each other and set the parameters for
what was amusing. We have phrases in the culture like 'sacred cow',
and cultures do more or less work out what we may and may not find
amusing. The notion that humour is somehow transgressive – that
whenever one's being amusing or amused, one is at least testing the
rules, if not actually breaking them – is a modern one. One is finding
out where the punishment might come from, and it is as though – in,
for instance, the terrible televised humiliations they have in Japan, or that
we can now see on TV programmes like *Big Brother* – it has already been
agreed by a large group of people with quite a lot of money that these
people should be ridiculed, and want to be. And there is an audience
for such things.
    The most difficult thing to work out is exactly what it is people
feel so guilty about that they want to participate in these spectacles.
We might hope that there are some subterranean political things going
on here, that somewhere people do feel very bad about their political
complicities, that they do feel greedy compared with the third world,
they do feel they're part of systems they can't wholly condone, they are
mindful of the fact that people suffer on the one hand as real criminals,
and on the other hand as political criminals. What constitutes the group

of punishable people is quite interesting. At one end, we've got child abusers, rapists, murderers of children; and at the other, we've got political dissidents; and, in the middle, all of us who haven't actually done any of those things, but feel guilty about something and clearly want to watch people being humiliated.

We have to make this funny, because if it weren't, we couldn't bear the spectacle. If you imagine one of these programmes, and suddenly you turn off the amusement button, you'd have a real catastrophe on your hands in terms of what you are witnessing.

UO *Why are we laughing at these people when we are presumably sharing their guilt?*

AP What would be doing if we weren't laughing? Being amused might be another form of unconsciously motivated narrow-mindedness. As long as we laugh we are OK, and as long as we are laughing, we aren't going to be feeling a whole range of

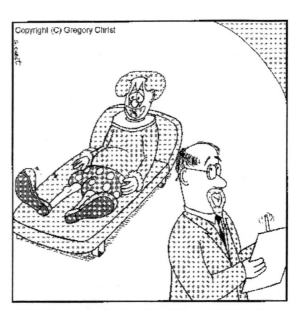

Copyright (C) Gregory Christ

Doc, I'm starting to wonder if they're still laughing WITH me, or AT me...

other things that are much more troubling. If I can make this amusing or feel amused about it, I won't have to feel ashamed, embarrassed, sad, grief-stricken, frantic or troubled. One of the things about laughter is that it is a kind of invulnerable state. In a curious way, one feels quite powerful and safe when one is laughing.

UO   *What do you feel about the ability to laugh at oneself?*

AP   Having the ability to laugh at yourself means two things. One, that you don't take yourself too seriously, and two, that you don't tyrannise over yourself and other people. But if you don't take yourself seriously enough, it's as though you offer yourself up to be disparaged and ridiculed by yourself and others. That is debilitating for everyone involved.

UO   *So all the things that you are saying about humour, including laughing at oneself, are about trying to avoid the sadomasochistic situation?*

AP   Yes. I can only feel strong if I'm making someone else feel weak. I can only be amused so long as somebody else is being humiliated. If we understood more about humour and the ways in which it is used, it would enable us to understand a lot of other things that go on around it and within it. ❏

Adam Phillips *is a writer and psychoanalyst. His latest book is* Promises, Promises, *published by Faber & Faber, 2000*

MARTIN ROWSON

Seriously funny

Is this funny?

An old Jewish tailor wins £5 million on the lottery, and throws a big party for all his friends and family to celebrate. Halfway through the evening he stands up and calls for silence.

'I'd just like to say a few words,' he says, 'to thank everyone who means most to me on this wonderful occasion. Obviously, my darling wife Esther, my beautiful children Max, Ruth and little David, my wonderful grandchildren, my friend and business partner Morrie, all my dear dear friends, and last but not least, Heinrich Himmler.'

A sharp intake of breath is heard from the crowd of well-wishers and merrymakers. 'What the hell are you saying, Abie?' a voice cries out. 'Why in God's name thank that bastard Himmler?'

'Well,' says Abie, pulling back his sleeve to reveal the tattooed numbers on his forearm, 'he gave me my lucky winning numbers …'

Or this?

Rastus comes home one night to find Liza in bed with another woman. He storms out of the room and rushes downstairs where, a few seconds later, Liza finds him in the kitchen with the fridge door open and his prick in a bowl of custard.

'Rastus!' Liza shrieks, 'what the hell are you doing?'

'Liza,' Rastus replies, 'I'm fuckin' dis custard!'

Or this?

A roofless prison building is seen from above. Its four walls contain neither windows nor doors; within those walls the inmates have formed a human pyramid to allow at least one of their number to reach high enough to see over the enclosing walls to the world outside.

Thing is, the man at the top of the pile is blind …

Maybe all of them, in their different ways, are funny. Maybe none. Maybe it's just the way I tell them. But let's look at those jokes more carefully, working on the premise that humour is, ultimately, a serious business. The joke about the Jewish tailor was told to me by a Jew and I, in turn, have told it to other Jews. We've all laughed. Is it then funny because we implicitly acknowledge its therapeutic value? That in response to the unspeakable horror of the Holocaust, the only options are tears, laughter or silence in the face of the unspeakable? And that the response of laughter is the most effective? In this instance the laughter invoked is not frivolous, but instead, faced with the defining murderous and inhuman act of the century, we stare into the abyss but succeed in maintaining our humanity by the very act of our laughter. The most basic of human responses defines, if you like, our humanity and, put bluntly, it means that we've won and the Nazis have lost. But what if that joke was told by an anti-Semite, or even a Nazi? At this point it's worth remembering that Hitler, according to many contemporary observers used to the traditions of German pedagogy, was so effective because he *was funny*. Does it, then, matter who tells a joke, or to whom it's told? Is a joke itself morally neutral?

What about the second joke? Needless to say, this wasn't told to me by an African-American, but by someone in the playground at school. Again, its background is one of horror: slavery, segregation, the demonising of African-Americans as rapacious sexual monsters and their objectification and degradation in the eyes of their white oppressors as subhuman clowns who talk funny. None the less, it is a very good, if pretty stupid pun, at which level it's very funny. That said, can you reasonably ignore all the other levels implicit in the joke?

The third joke isn't really fair, as it's my description of a cartoon drawn by a Romanian dissident cartoonist during the horrors of Ceauşescu's tyranny. As a response to those horrors, it's an entirely valid and pertinent comment, but it isn't funny at all.

Of course, cultural and historical distinctions apply. There's an old Peter Cook and Dudley Moore sketch where Pete and Dud are wandering round the National Gallery and Dud's just been to see the Leonardo cartoon, but can't see the joke, to which Pete replies that the sense of humour changes over the years. 'I bet the Medici were pissing themselves at that one.' In the cultural sphere, the rest of the world looks on in stony-faced bemusement – but not amusement – as the French laugh themselves stupid at the mugging antics of Jerry Lewis. But is there, then, an ur-humour? Something we can identify as the universal bedrock uniting humanity in its capacity for laughter?

Stripped down to its essentials, I think all humour can be defined as laughing at farting and the people you hate. Any baby, if you make a farting noise at it, will laugh. This seems to be innate, although you can then begin to build cultural constructs on top of that. Jokes about farting, shit and sex are universal, although it's difficult to say at what point the intrinsically hilarious nature of the noise made by the squidgy substances that issue from our bodies becomes overlaid, in our response to it, by our cultural conditioning: in other words, when do we start using laughter as a defence mechanism to help us cope with our taboos?

Hatred, of course, is an easier one to pin down. *Schadenfreude* is an innate and universal human phenomenon. Jokes about the stupidity of people different from you seems a pretty effective – and enjoyable if hardly harmless – way of reinforcing the social cohesion of your tribe. Thus the English laugh at the stupidity of the Irish, while the Irish laugh at the stupidity of Kerrymen, and so on.

Of course, in comedy, timing is everything. Compare our public and private responses to disasters. When famines or earthquakes or massacres are reported in the media, we want sensitivity, solemnity and poignancy, while simultaneously, in our daily lives, we hear and repeat the most appallingly sick jokes about exactly the same things. Given the speed with which what we might term 'folk humour' percolates into the culture, one's almost inclined to think that governments employ teams of gag writers in secret, underground bunkers, poised to hand the latest reworking of a joke about Biafra to squads of special agents, who then infiltrate the general population. With this safety valve, we are thus prevented from all going mad at the insupportable horror of everything. The point is, we want to laugh and cry, and that is entirely human. While, for instance, Diana Spencer's brilliantly stage-managed funeral made millions feel magnificently miserable, the jokes that made the same millions of people guffaw in pubs and offices were in general circulation within 48 hours of her death.

I'm lucky to work as a political cartoonist in a country where what I do is so firmly entrenched in the cultural landscape that I can act pretty much with impunity. In my time I've drawn, I hope, some truly cruel, offensive and totally unfair cartoons of British and international

politicians. Even the notoriously cowardly sensitivities of newspaper editors recognise that I should be given licence to articulate things visually that would be completely unacceptable if merely written down in an article. But what I'm doing is ostensibly 'humorous', and therefore not to be taken too seriously, even if deadly serious in intent. My get-out clause will always be that anyone who doesn't like it 'can't take a joke': for democratic politicians to admit in public that they appear to have no sense of humour would be the kiss of death, particularly in a country as proud of its collective 'sense of humour' as Britain.

In fact, the worst I can expect from a politician is that he'll buy the original of the cartoon I've drawn attacking him, when I was hoping it would force him to resign in disgrace. Generally, humour can be seen as an instinctive response to deal with the human condition. In the area of satire, however, humour becomes part of an altogether more institutionalised dialectic. As a political cartoonist, I use humour as a tool to propagate my own political agenda, but in doing so, in Britain at least, I'm cemented into a kind of contract with my victims, where we cancel each other out, but also where each side recognises the importance of the other, and has done for hundreds of years. In the late eighteenth century, the great satirical caricaturist James Gillray was badgered for

months by George Canning, later foreign secretary but then an up-and-coming and extremely ambitious young politician, to be put into one of Gillray's prints. For months Gillray refused, until finally he drew Canning as a corpse hanging from a gas lamp in a print showing what London would look like under the Jacobin Terror.

On the basis that all publicity is good publicity, Canning clearly understood that Gillray's endorsement proved him sufficiently important to merit attention, while Gillray understood equally strongly that it was his job to keep Canning in his place by making him look ridiculous. If you like, satire is tolerated as a safety valve by democratic politicians, as just another humiliation to suffer along with having to prostitute themselves in order to get elected, and then prostitute themselves further in order to win advancement. All in all, it's a small price to pay. Later, Canning coerced Gillray to produce a whole series of pro-government propaganda prints for Canning's paper *The Anti-Jacobin*, often diametrically at odds with the political attitudes evinced in his previous work.

And yet the worm remained in the bud. In a shamelessly propagandist print of a giant John Bull grappling with Napoleon across the globe, Gillray showed his real feelings by subtitling it 'Fighting over the Dung-Heap' (returning us, incidentally, to shit). The satirist may have had the last laugh over the politician, but so what? Satirists may fulfil the role of court jester, but never forget that the king is still the king.

Which begs the question, when does satire actually work? In my more pretentious moments, I like to think that, in pointing up the idiocy and venality of those in power, I'm engaged in corrective surgery, albeit with a cudgel. If they've got any sense, they laugh it off. Even during John Major's Conservative government after 1992, satirists – supposedly enjoying a golden age – were, in fact, responding to the overwhelming public perception that the government was a busted flush, and just joined everyone else in pelting fish in a barrel with custard pies. How, after all, do you satirise a government which gave us the BSE crisis? – when, as a matter of policy and free-marketeering dogma, it deregulated the slaughterhouses to the point where cattle were turned into cannibals, rendering the national dish, the Roast Beef of Old England, not only poisonous but guaranteed to drive you mad before you died. They then compounded this by declaring a 'war' on our major trading partners because of their refusal to eat our deadly cows. It almost seemed that the most outrageous, disgusting and ridiculous policy any satirist could imagine would be trumped by the Tories, like Ann Widdecombe demanding that female prisoners in labour be shackled to their bedsteads. You couldn't make it up. More to the point, Hogarth and Swift couldn't have made it up either. This was meta-satire, beyond satire and, as Tom Lehrer said when Henry Kissinger received the Nobel Peace Prize: 'Satire is dead.'

Except, of course, that satire is never dead, and its effectiveness can be gauged by the response of the satirised. The great British twentieth-century cartoonist David Low was generally recognised during World War II as one of the most effective anti-Nazi propagandists because, rather than rendering the Nazis as sinister (which they certainly were) he made them, to quote a Tory MP at the time, 'look like bloody fools'. It got Low on to the Gestapo death list, which is praise indeed. Then again, the last cartoonist to be imprisoned in Britain was the cartoonist for *Bulldog*, the newspaper of the fascist British Movement, who was sent down in the mid-eighties for incitement to racial hatred. And we're back to Hitler's jokes, and the moral neutrality of humour.

Humour is a blunt but double-edged instrument. As a cartoonist I'm part of a long tradition of 'taking the piss' out of my social superiors and political leaders that has characterised the majority of people probably for ever (note our return to the eternal hilarity of bodily functions).

William Hogarth did the same. Personally, Hogarth typified the xenophobic, conservative bourgeois attitudes of his time. And yet, even when at his most morally polemical, he couldn't resist taking the piss. Thus, in the Guildhall Banquet print from his series 'The Idle and Industrious Apprentice', in a scene that was meant to show the rewards of hard work (in a series of cheap, popular prints intended to be hung in workshops to provide an uplifting example), we don't focus on the Industrious Apprentice in the background, newly elected Sheriff of the City of London, but on the group of swinish City burghers pigging themselves at the trough in the foreground. Hogarth, like Swift and Gillray, was showing the blood and shit and piss that lurks beneath the finest exterior, and that those who proclaim themselves the best of us are the same potential sack of corruption and decay as those they deem the worst. Throughout the 1980s, the knowledge that Margaret Thatcher was having a shit when the Brighton bomb exploded never failed to offer me some hope of salvation for us all.

And that, finally, is the point, if not the explanation, of humour. Nothing, and no one, is sacred. But look at the flip side of that just before your sides split at the hilarity of it all. Take, for example, the reaction against political correctness. I assume that those people who consider political correctness to be the greatest tyranny we currently strain under have just forgotten to say that, actually, they want a return to their previously untrammelled freedom to call blacks niggers, Jews Yids, gays poofs and women whores; and if any of those groups object, it's simply because they 'can't take a joke'. Perhaps the simple fact of making that observation marks me down as an insufferably solemn, humourless bore. But to me some things are sacred, even if they aren't to you. That's a political argument, not one about comedy. And although I don't find jokes made by the powerful about the powerless particularly funny, nor the way the powerful have and will silence and often murder the powerless for making jokes about them, maybe it's just the way they tell them. Humour, like all other weapons, is used by people, and aimed at other people, for their own ends. My response, ultimately, is the same as the one I use when one of my children makes a hopelessly bad or feeble joke, and which never fails to make them roll about in helpless laughter for hours on end. 'Laugh? I nearly shat.' ❏

Martin Rowson *is a cartoonist and writer*

By any, many names

Burlesque That species of literary composition or dramatic representation which aims at exciting laughter by caricature of serious works, or by grotesque imitation of what is meant to be dignified.
First used in the US to describe 'that portion of a Negro minstrel entertainment which contains dialogue and sketches'. Now most frequently used as a more salubrious term for a striptease.

Caricature A grotesque or ludicrous representation of a person or thing, by exaggeration of his, her or its most characteristic and striking features.
First used by the Scottish author Tobias George Smollett, who in 1749 modestly declared: 'It would be caricaturing the peerage to confer it on me.'

Cartoon A humorous or topical drawing (of any size) in a newspaper or periodical, which, by the devices of caricature, analogy and ludicrous juxtaposition, produces a comic effect.
Up until the 19th century, the word was commonly used as a term to describe 'a drawing on stout paper'. The first use of the word in the modern sense came in 1843, when the British satirical journal Punch announced that, in an ensuing volume, the magazine would 'astonish the Parliamentary Committee' with 'the publication of several exquisite designs, to be called cartoons'.

Clown A fool or jester, who entertains by jokes, antics and tricks, usually as a character on stage, in a harlequinade, or in a circus.
Originated as a disparaging term. It was first used in the 16th century as a label for a churl: a person of rustic origin 'without refinement or culture; an ignorant, rude, uncouth, crass and ill-bred man'.

Comedy A stage play or narrative of a light and amusing character, which adopts a humorous or familiar style with a happy conclusion to its plot.
Dante's magnum opus, the Divine Comedy, completed just before the Italian poet's death in 1321, was thus titled because, 'in the conclusion, it is prosperous, pleasant and desirable', and because stylistically it was 'written in the vulgar tongue, in which women and children speak'.

Farce A light dramatic work, marked by coarse violence, irreverent buffoonery and an improbable plot, which has for its sole object to excite laughter.
The genre developed in 15th-century France, where actors attempted to invigorate traditional religious plays by inserting acrobatic displays and impromptu sketches into the performance. The word 'farce', meaning 'stuffing', was used to describe how the script was literally crammed with these extra scenes.

Fool A person deficient in judgement or sense, who acts or behaves stupidly, or one who professionally counterfeits folly for the entertainment of others.
Although appearing most commonly in Elizabethan literature, the origins of the professional fool can be traced to pre-Christian times. Often deformed or crippled, fools flourished in ancient Egypt, where, believing that the disfigured could avert evil, the pharaohs kept them for good luck as well as for entertainment.

Humour An action, speech or piece of writing that amuses, characterised by oddity, jocularity, facetiousness, comicality or fun.
Derived from the word's first usage in medieval physiology. In the Middle Ages, it was asserted that the body was constituted of four 'humours': blood, choler, phlegm and bile. With the four in equilibrium, a person was said to possess 'the perfect temperament', characterised by happiness, generosity and amorousness.

Irony A form of humour, ridicule or light sarcasm in which the intended meaning of a speech is the opposite of that expressed by the words used.
From the Greek eironeia, used to describe 'the Socratic method of discussion, marked by the speaker's profession of ignorance'.

Joke A humorous anecdote, remark or activity, designed to evoke laughter or amusement.
From the Latin word iocus, meaning a sport or trifle.

Knockabout A boisterous practical joke or rowdy comic performance.
Originally an Australian term for a rugged casual labourer, often involved in street fights and brawls. Now used to describe a performance that is characterised by comic violence.

Lampoon A virulent or scurrilous satire upon an individual.

From the French verb lamper, *meaning to booze or guzzle alcohol.*

Mime A kind of simple farcical drama (usually without words), characterised by mimicry, gesticulation and the ludicrous representation of familiar types of character.

The modern, purely silent, form of mime was developed in the 17th century, and described by Marcel Marceau, its chief twentieth-century purveyor, as 'the art of expressing feelings by attitudes and not a means of expressing words through gestures'. Mime acts in ancient Rome and Greece included dialogue and song, and sometimes saw convicted criminals being put to death on stage as part of the performance.

Mirth Gaiety of mind, as manifested in jest, laughter, merriment and hilarity.

The word has its roots in medieval times, when it was used to describe a state of religious ecstasy attained through worship.

Parody A composition in prose or verse in which the style and characteristic turns of thought and phrase of an author or authors are closely imitated to make them appear ridiculous.

The first recorded example of parody is the anonymous ancient Greek work Batrachomyomachia, *translated as 'The Battle of the Frogs and Mice'. Written in Homeric verse, the composition mocked the epic style of* The Iliad *and* The Odyssey.

Satire A literary composition in which prevailing vices or follies are held up to ridicule through the employment of irony, satire and lampoon.

Satire possesses a distinguished tradition in the field of dissent. As early as 1599, the Archbishop of Canterbury and the Bishop of London issued a joint order prohibiting the publishing of satire and instructing local authorities to incinerate all satirical works. Samuel Johnson noted the potency of satire as a form of criticism when he commented, 'abuse is not so dangerous when there is no vehicle of wit or delicacy, nor subtle conveyance'.

Sitcom A humorous drama series featuring the reactions of a regular cast of characters to unusual situations, such as misunderstandings or embarrassing coincidences.

The term 'sitcom' is an amalgam of the words 'situation' and 'comedy'. Although most commonly
associated with television, the earliest example of the genre, a show called Amos 'n' Andy, could be found on the wireless in the USA in the 1930s.

Skit A quizzing or satirical reflection on a person or thing, usually in the form of a theatrical performance.

First used in 16th-century Scotland as a term for 'a wanton, vain or frivolous woman'.

Slapstick A boisterous form of comedy marked by crude jokes, horseplay and physical action.

In early pantomime, a slapstick (a wooden instrument that produced a slapping effect) was used to simulate the sound of a punch or heavy blow. This device lent its name to the genre.

Spoof A skit or 'send-up'; specifically a film, play or other work that satirises a particular genre.

Originally the name of a mysterious card game that was revived in the 1880s by British comedian Arthur Roberts. The game was described as one of 'trickery and nonsense'.

Stand-up An act involving a performer delivering a comic monologue or succession of jokes to an audience.

First used in the USA in the 1960s, after cabaret bars started hiring comedians to entertain their clientele.

Vaudeville A play or stage performance of a light and amusing character, interspersed with songs.

Forbidden from performing traditional theatre pieces by the royal acting company's stranglehold on 'serious drama', amateur and semi-professional companies in 18th-century France were restricted to staging comedies and light entertainment. The term 'vaudeville' came to describe this genre.

Ventriloquism The art of speaking sounds in such a manner that the voice appears to proceed from some person or object other than the speaker.

Formed from an amalgam of the Latin words venter *and* loqui, *meaning 'belly-speak'.*

Wit The ability to perceive and express in an ingeniously humorous manner the relationship between seemingly incongruous or disparate things.

Wit is seen very much as the thinking man's humour; it requires a 'quickness of intellect' and 'liveliness of fancy' to be fully appreciated. ❏

DG

Satire

I'll publish, right or wrong:
Fools are my theme, let satire be my song
Lord Byron

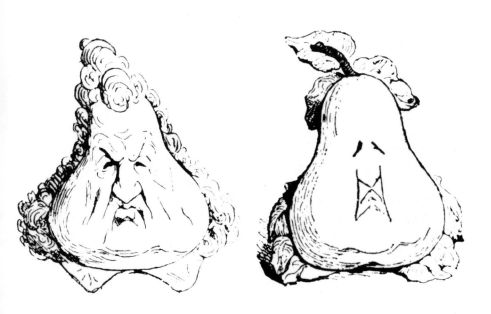

Charles Philipon (1806–62), King Louis Philippe as a pear, *1831, pen and ink drawing.*

In French, 'poire' ('pear') is slang for 'idiot'.

EDWARD LUCIE-SMITH

The satirical eye

Caricatures call into question the men and manners of the world they depict. Little wonder that caricaturists and those in power have so long been at odds

Caricature is a divided and, to some extent also, a socially divisive concept. The term itself derives from the Italian verb *caricare* – to load, or surcharge, with exaggerated detail. The first caricatures in this sense are usually said to have been made by Italian artists of the seventeenth century, such as Annibale Carracci and Gianlorenzo Bernini, who acquired the habit of dashing off exaggerated sketches of their contemporaries. These sketches were simultaneously mocking and flattering – flattering in the sense that a good caricature implies that the person who made it has given close and loving attention to the appearance of his subject. Where they portray a known individual, rather than a type, they tend to enhance rather than diminish his or her importance.

In fact, these exaggerated portraits are only a specialised offshoot of a much longer, broader and more important tradition – that of making humorous and satirical visual allegories. Unlike portrait caricatures, these allegories are often fiercely resented by those at whom they are directed, and more than one artist working in this vein has been persecuted for his pains. The history of these designs can be traced to remote antiquity – there are humorous drawings of animals behaving like human beings in certain Ancient Egyptian papyri. The thing which really gave them their impetus, however, was the invention of printing. In particular, the polemicists of the Reformation made full use of them. A famous example, from the Catholic side, shows *The Devil Playing Luther as a Pair of Bagpipes*. In this the fleshy features of the great religious

Erhard Schoen (1491–1542), The Devil Playing Luther as a Pair of Bagpipes, 1521, woodcut with body colour.

reformer are converted into the bellows of the musical instrument. There are several things which are significant about the design. One is its concision. It makes its point immediately, far more rapidly than any written text, however brilliantly phrased. Another is the way in which it takes leave of any commitment to realism. Fantastic metaphorical images of this sort were not an invention of sixteenth-century printmakers. They had already enjoyed a long history as decorations in the margins of medieval manuscripts, and (in three-dimensional form) as subsidiary carved decorations in churches, such as roof bosses, carvings on misericords and other ornaments.

However, at a time when art was moving towards a commitment to realism, satirical designs of this sort resisted the tendency. They increasingly became one of the bulwarks of resistance against literal depiction. Within the history of caricature, from this time onwards, we find the seeds of some of the tendencies which were to be the hallmarks of Modernism in art – Surrealism on the one hand, Expressionism on the other. The portrayal of Luther would be recognised by most people

Giovanni Lorenzo Bernini (1598–1680), Caricature of a Captain in the Army of Urban VIII, *1644, pen and ink on paper.*

as proto-Surrealist; the personal caricatures made by Carracci, Bernini and others anticipate Expressionist treatments of the human figure, omitting only the ingredient of anguish.

I think one can also say that caricatures played an important part in teaching people to look in new ways at what surrounded them. People often talk of the influence on ways of seeing exercised first by photography, then by film and television. Many of these lessons were anticipated by the caricaturists, especially in the great age of caricature which ran from the 1780s until the end of the nineteenth century. I can offer two especially telling examples: one is the work of the Englishman James Gillray; the other that of a French pioneer of political caricature, Charles Philipon. Gillray's *Fashionable Contrasts: or The Duchess's little Shoe yielding to the Magnitude of the Duke's Foot* belongs to a time when the English royal family was even more savagely treated in the popular media than it sometimes is now. His subjects here are the then Duke and Duchess of York. Gillray sums up the marital and sexual relationship of the couple through an employment of close-up which anticipates the use modern photographers have made of this device. His design, like photographic close-ups, encourages the viewer to construct the complete scene for himself, using the fragments he has been given. Gillray performs a visual conjuring trick: he avoids depicting something which, if shown in full, would undoubtedly have got him into trouble, and which, in any case, would have been an affront to the social

Agostino Carracci (1557–1602), Caricature of Rabbatin de Griffi and his wife Spilla Pomina, pen and ink on paper. Credit: Nationalmuseum, Stockholm/Bridgeman Art Library, London

conventions of his day. At the same time, he gets his audience to identity imaginatively with his comment on the situation by making them participants rather than just spectators.

Philipon's image (pp32–33) is not fragmentary but sequential. It shows the portrait of the then reigning monarch, King Louis Philippe, being transformed by gradual stages into the image of a pear. In French, '*poire*' ('pear') is slang for 'idiot'. The technique is rather like the kind of cinematic dissolve where one object or scene gradually turns into another. To this is added the force of the verbal/visual pun. Philipon was the founder of the satirical journal *La Caricature* whose birth coincided with that of the July Monarchy in 1830. One of the draughtsmen he employed was Honoré Daumier, a much greater artist than himself. Daumier, in turn, made full use of the relatively new printing technique, lithography, which enabled artists to set down their thoughts in exceptionally fresh and immediate form. The fact that Louis Philippe's government, in general fairly tolerant in terms of its time, actually imprisoned Daumier for a six-month period in 1832 was a tribute both to the savagery and to the effectiveness of his attacks.

As it happens, there is a twist in the tail of this story. Sentenced to six months, Daumier spent only two of them in prison, but the other

James Gillray (1757–1815), caricature of the Duke and Duchess of York, 1792. Credit: AKG, London

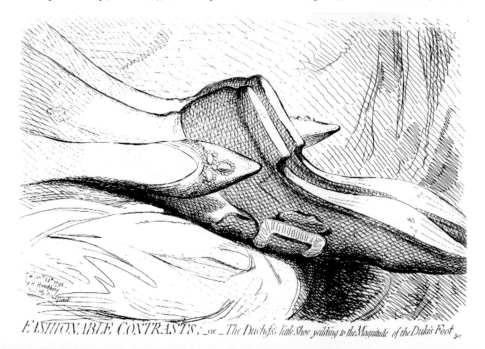

F ISHIONABLE CONTRASTS; _ or _ The Duchess's little Shoe yeilding to the Magnitude of the Duke's Foot _

Honoré Daumier (1808–79), La rue Transnonain, le 15 avril, *lithograph, July 1834. French government troops, sent to quell riots in a working-class quarter of Paris, massacre a sleeping family. Credit: AKG, London*

four in a mental hospital. This, of course, reminds one now of the punishments meted out under communism to certain Russian dissidents, though their treatment was in general much more severe. It also seems to offer a comment on the fundamental nature of caricature itself. The wounded Louis Philippe was not wrong to see the activity as a kind of madness. Far more than purely verbal attacks, certain caricatures alter and destabilise the world whose folly and wickedness they attempt to depict. They frequently suggest that appearances are fluid, that one condition of being can dissolve into another. Such transformations may provoke laughter at one level, but they also induce anxiety at another and deeper one. Caricatures, in other words, sometimes actually call into question the quotidian solidity of the world they depict. If we look at the matter in Freudian terms, we note that many political actions seem to have as their primary concern the relief of anxiety – that of those who govern, but also that of those who are governed. Censorship can often be seen as a means of attempting to do this – of restoring stability to a situation which seems to be in danger of losing it. In the circumstances, can we be surprised that caricaturists and those in power are so frequently at odds with one another? ❏

Edward Lucie-Smith *is a writer and art critic. His most recent book is* Flesh and Stone, *published by Ipso Facto, 2000*

JERRY ROBINSON

The American cartoon

'Stop them damn pictures'

Without Europe, there would probably be no distinct US style in cartoons and humour, says a well-known US cartoonist

Benjamin Franklin was the first American cartoonist and father of its humorous literature. As Franklin observed: 'Pieces of pleasantry and mirth have a secret charm in them to allay the heats and tumults of our spirits and to make man forget his restless resentments.' Franklin, along with Paul Revere, another early patriot of considerable and versatile artistic talents, drew cartoons to resemble British tyranny. It was Franklin's drawing of a snake severed in as many pieces as there were colonies, with the motto 'Join, or Die' that was the most effective symbol in urging the colonies to unite against the British.

An English émigré, Frank Leslie, brought the graphic humour magazine to America in 1863. There proved to be a growing market for humorous literature and cartoons, nurturing writers such as Artemus Ward, Josh Billings and Mark Twain, and cartoonists like Ed Jump, Livingstone Hopkins and Frederick Opper. Comic lithography and portfolios were popular and widely published, notably those by Currier and Ives.

US political cartooning of the nineteenth century was for the most part confined to almanacs and satirical weeklies, such as *Leslie's Illustrated Weekly* and *Harper's Weekly*. There was widespread use of satire with classical and Shakespearean illusions. The style was of European origin, as were most of the leading cartoonists of the day. Nast was Bavarian;

Benjamin Franklin, cartoon in the Pennsylvania Gazette, *9 May 1754. The eight colonies are shown in roughly geographical position along America's east coast, with the snake's head pointing north.*

Joseph Keppler was Viennese; William Newman was British, as were the Gillam brothers. Joseph Keppler came to America and founded *Puck* (1877). It was *Puck*, *Judge* (1881) and *Life* (1883) that gave birth to a new age in American graphic humour. Cartoons by AB Frost, TS Sullivant, Walt McDougall, SD Ehrhart and Frederick Opper exemplified the mixture of accurate observation and a love of the ridiculous, elegant and, at times, even crude and vulgar, that established the social cartoon as a mixture in US literature. The *New Yorker*, founded in 1925, refined the traditional 'he and she' jokes into the succinct one-liner, and has become identified with a particular style of sophisticated cartoon. Among the early contributors were James Thurber with his war between the sexes, floppy dogs and walruses; George Price with his dowager duchesses of cold water, flat society and unkempt middle-aged gallants; and William Steig with his philosophic small fry. While the *New Yorker* set the standard for the urbane cartoon with the art of Peter Arno, Charles Addams and Saul Steinberg, over the decades the genre became an integral part of virtually every popular magazine, such as the *Saturday*

Evening Post, Colliers, Ladies Home Journal, Esquire and *Playboy*. They nurtured a dazzling array of individual stylists.

While humour has been an integral part of the fabric of US life, from time to time even our democratic institutions have been inhospitable to satire, particularly in times of crisis. A crisis for politicians is when they feel violated by political cartoonists, and they have often retaliated with attempts to silence their tormentors. 'Stop them damn pictures,' cried the infamous 'Boss' Tweed in anguish over the unrelenting and savage attacks by the ubiquitous Thomas Nast. 'I don't care a straw for your newspaper articles. My constituents can't read. But they can't help seeing them damn pictures!' In desperation, Tweed, who led Tammany Hall and the band of rogues who controlled New York City from 1866

THE "BRAINS"

Thomas Nast, The Brains of the Tweed Ring, lithograph, 1871. Tweed, boss of the notoriously corrupt Tammany Hall (headquarters of the New York Democratic Party), was brought down in part by the strength of Nast's cartoons.

to 1871, tried to bribe the incorruptible cartoonist with half a million dollars to 'study art in Europe'. Nast continued his scathing ridicule. Score one for the cartoonist. That time the politicians went to jail.

However, Tweed bribed his way out and fled to Europe. In an ironic twist of fate, a Spanish official recognised Tweed from Nast's caricature in *Harper's Weekly*. Tweed was arrested and extradited. His baggage was found to contain a complete set of Nast's cartoons, except for the one which was to send him to jail. Nast's rich legacy includes the symbols of the Republican elephant, Tammany Tiger, and the US portrayal of Santa Claus. Humour in times of insanity is what keeps us sane. It is also what keeps us free. There is nothing that tyrants and rascals fear more than satire and ridicule, and the graphic form has always proved to be uniquely painful. Freedom of expression for the political cartoonist is a litmus test for democracy. Totalitarian regimes rarely tolerate cartoon satire of their leaders – at least not until they are deposed or deceased.

While newspaper cartoons appeared throughout the nineteenth century, it was not until the 1870s that the New York *Daily Graphic* became the first newspaper regularly to feature cartoons. Walt McDougall's 'The Royal Feast of Belshazzar', printed on the front page of the New York *World* during the presidential campaign of 1884, established the editorial cartoon as a regular feature in US newspapers. McDougall's cartoon, as well as the series 'The Tattooed Man' by Bernard Gillam, was credited with electing Grover Cleveland in one of the most bitterly contested of presidential races.

It has been noted that a good caricature is only fully appreciated by those who have been its victims. Occasionally politicians are its beneficiaries. 'Two things elected me,' acknowledged President Grant, 'the swords of Sheridan and the pencil of Thomas Nast.' By 1906, there was a newspaper in every major US city, and the political cartoon proved an equally powerful force in local, state and national politics.

The transition into the twentieth century brought spectacular and profound changes to US society that gave it lusty vitality. It was an era of emigrants from Europe swarming to our shores, the Irish, Germans, Russians, Swedes, Italians, Catholics and Jews and others fleeing persecution whose strange customs and accents were the delight of vaudeville comedians. This was the cultural stew that nourished a new art form that proved to be of unprecedented vigour and longevity. The US and the comic strip were made for each other.

Many of the first wave of strip cartoonists were themselves immigrants or first-generation Americans. Rudolph Dirks, creator of *The Katzenjammer Kids*, was born in Germany; Frederick Burr Opper, son of an Austrian immigrant, contributed *Happy Hooligan* and *Alphonse and Gaston*. Immigrant and racial themes were the basis for much of the humour. It was the time of Lew Dockstader's black minstrels and the German dialect of Weber and Fields. Comic art was not immune. And as times changed, US society found new generations of diverse comic geniuses to interpret it. They range from Richard Outcault (*The Yellow Kid*), George Herriman (*Krazy Kat*), Winsor McCay (*Little Nemo*), Elzie Segar (*Popeye*) and Walt Disney (*Mickey Mouse*) to Al Capp (*Li'l Abner*), Chic Young (*Blondie*), Walt Kelley (*Pogo*), Mort Walker (*Beetle Bailey*), Charles Schultz (*Peanuts*), Bill Watterson (*Calvin and Hobbes*), Joe Schuster and Jerry Siegel (*Superman*), Stan Lee (*Spiderman*) and Robert Crumb (*Mr Natural*).

If there is a US style in cartoon and humour distinguishable from others, it cannot be considered without paying homage to cultural influences from abroad. To ignore one is not fully to understand the other. ❏

Jerry Robinson is a cartoonist and founder of the Cartoonists and Writers Syndicate

Fritz the Cat: one of Robert Crumb's greatest cartoons

KEVIN KWONG

Tung in cheek

There are few places in Asia where a publisher can openly satirise a government leader without fear of being put behind bars

Contrary to what its publisher may insist on, Hong Kong's latest satire *Lo Mung Tung* (Old Senile Managing Director) is all about you-know-who. The jokes are so blatant it is hard to miss the innuendo.

The character Lo Mung Tung is, as his name suggests, old and senile. He heads and runs a corporate business, known simply as 'The Firm', where he is surrounded by a bunch of losers. His wife is a formidable shopper and his grey hair is cut in a crop. He is obsessed with the figure '85,000' – a reference to the on-off housing provision target perhaps? – and the 'third party', the person alleged to have pressured Dr Robert Chung Ting-yiu to stop conducting opinion polls on the popularity of the head of our government.

OK. We'll say it: Lo Mung Tung is a caricature of the Chief Executive of the Hong Kong Special Administrative Region, Tung Chee-hwa.

'No, he isn't,' reiterates the book's publisher, Jimmy Pang Chiming. 'Lo Mung Tung's surname is Lo. He is just some managing director of a company who happens to make very bad decisions because the advisers around him are totally incompetent. It's not our intention to offend or be disrespectful. The book is just for laughs. It's not intended to be political.'

He says the idea for the book came from his writer friends who simply wanted to have their jokes published, and they thought this was great material. 'And I wanted a gimmick to attract people to my stall at the Hong Kong Book Fair,' Pang says.

It did. Since *Lo Mung Tung*, costing only HK$25 (US$3.50) a copy, appeared at the book fair in July, where 600 copies sold out in double-quick time, its sales have been phenomenal. The initial print run of 15,000 copies sold out in a week. An incredible feat considering that local fiction that sells between 1,000 and 2,000 copies in a year is considered a huge success.

'Its popularity has taken us completely by surprise,' Pang says. 'To be honest, I was so busy that week I didn't even read what was in the book.' The fact that the 44-year-old former scriptwriter put up a mock 'censored' sign at his stall urging people to buy a copy 'before it's banned' no doubt helped fuel sales.

So far, *Lo Mung Tung* has sold around 40,000 first-edition copies and has made between HK$100,000 and HK$200,000 profits for Sub-Culture Publishing. Not bad for a book that was put together ten days before going to press. Pang then followed up with *Lo Mung Tung and Lo Mung Tai* (Old Senile Managing Director and Old Senile Wife). It had a 'conservative' 30,000 print run.

You need to know your current affairs pretty well to be able to understand or appreciate the Lo Mung Tung jokes, and they don't translate well into English because they are mostly deft plays on Chinese characters and colloquialisms. For instance, Lo Mung Tung loves playing mah-jong, but will only win a game if he picks the *pat man ng* [85,000] tile – a reference to that housing provision target of 85,000 flats again. Since no such tile exists – there are only *pat man* [80,000] tiles in a mah-jong set – he will never win.

But here is a joke that is perfectly straightforward: Lo Mung Tung visits a psychiatric hospital and asks a patient whether he knows who he is. When the patient turns from side to side, Lo Mung Tung explains, 'I am the only managing director of The Firm. I'm its leader, its centre of power. I make important decisions, making sure everyone has a roof over their heads, improving people's living standards and saving our environment.' The patient gives him a smile of recognition: 'Quick, call the doctor, you are showing the same symptoms that brought me here.'

Even the author's pseudonym, Foo Chi Chan, as in negative assets or liability, is a reference to the government's policy of quashing rising property prices in the late 1990s, which subsequently left many home-buyers stuck with flats that had negative equity.

So who, exactly, is Foo Chi Chan? '*Lo Mung Tung* is actually the work of five different people who happen to be my writer friends,' Pang reveals. 'Foo Chi Chan is their collective name. Since all are moonlighting on this project, they will not be disclosing their identities.'

So their anonymity has nothing to do with the fact that they are satirising the Chief Executive? 'Absolutely not,' Pang says. 'The book is about social issues, not politics.' So is he one of the contributors? 'No, I am not,' he answers.

While Pang is still surprised by, and no doubt savouring, the book's success, he believes its appeal lies mainly in its ability to capture and react to the public mood. '*Lo Mung Tung* is not so much a social commentary as the voice of society. I'm not here to incite [public unrest],' he says, 'but readers find the content relevant and funny.'

Does the Chief Executive find the jokes funny? When asked whether he had read *Lo Mung Tung*, his office issued the following statement: 'As freedom of speech is enshrined in the Basic Law, we attach great importance to public opinion and are determined to ensure that government policies are in line with the views of the public.'

Pang insists the book is just good, clean fun. He says the jokes about Lo Mung Tung and his close circle of advisers are all written in good faith. 'No matter how dissatisfied we are with the Hong Kong government, we don't want anyone to step down ... at the moment; I don't think we can find anyone to replace [Tung Chee-hwa],' he says.

Pang's publishing house, Sub-Culture, publishes a mix of titles including *The Quotations of Li Kashing* and numerous romantic novels targeting schoolgirls. He is now planning to publish *Lo Mung Tung* as a monthly. 'It's a sad irony that there are authors out there who spend years writing a book that sells only 100 copies, while our books, which have less than 100 pages, just took off like this,' Pang adds. 'I feel kind of lucky.' ❑

Kevin Kwong is a freelance journalist based in Hong Kong

Clowns
& comics

In the end, everything is a gag
Charlie Chaplin

I was a bird – then I met this artist

KEN CAMPBELL

In the beginning

Tongues, gift of (also called Glossolalia)

'Utterances approximating words and speech, usually produced during states of intense religious excitement.'
Glossolalia first occurred among the followers of Jesus at Pentecost (Acts 2:4) when 'they were all filled with the Holy Spirit and began to speak in other tongues, as the Spirit gave them utterance'.

Three things led us to eventual Glossolalic ecstasy:
  1 Stanislav Szukalski's PROTONG notion – the proto-language spoken by all Humans (a–Humans at that time merely gibbered) before the Great Deluge.
  2 The inspired prince of some centuries agone who reckoned that if one-year-old kids were denied any adult presence, just given troughs of milk and had pasties thrown over the wall, they'd grow up naturally speaking Hebrew. That isn't what happens. What happens is they die. But inspiring that the bloke had the balls to properly test his theory.
  And 3 Jean Tardieu's speculation on THE LOST VOWEL.
  Of the three, I'd say the last was what led to the incredible event in the Hainault Forest Sea Scout Hut.

'I have followed vocalic sounds on their secular journeys,' says Jean Tardieu, 'I have hearkened across the ages to the roar of the A, the bleat of the E, the whistle of the I, the snore of the O, the hoot of the U … And now, almost at the end of my career, I still await, still anticipate, THE UNKNOWN VOWEL, the Vowel of Vowels that will contain all others … a Vowel that is both beginning and end, that will take all of a man's breath to pronounce, by a monstrous distension of the jaws, as though combining in a single cry the yawn of boredom, the howl of hunger, the moan of love and the rattle of death. When found, creation itself will be swallowed up and nothing will remain – nothing but THE UNKNOWN VOWEL.'

To find the unknown vowel. And to explode, or more likely, whimper away the entirety of creation, that's the galaxies, the lot. Or maybe set it into Time-reversed mode so you sit on the toilet and the poo goes up your bum and in the morning you cough up a neat-looking breakfast. Backwards to the pinpoint of creation. And maybe the discoverers of THE UNKNOWN VOWEL get to travel the full retro-journey squeezed down at the last (first!) moment to
Pllpop
into the Nothing

THE EXPERIMENT
VENUE Hainault Forest Sea Scout Hut. Saturday afternoon and evening, early summer 1955.
PRESENT Most of the first eleven cricket team (weirdly), about 30 of us in all, including me, Neville Plashwit Porter, Fish, Fish, Jaffe, Pfaff, Mattick, Meredith, Ion Will. Also Nina Plashwit (age 4¾).
GUEST Ralph Plashwit (Neville and Nina's Dad).

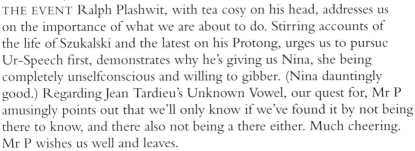

THE EVENT Ralph Plashwit, with tea cosy on his head, addresses us on the importance of what we are about to do. Stirring accounts of the life of Szukalski and the latest on his Protong, urges us to pursue Ur-Speech first, demonstrates why he's giving us Nina, she being completely unselfconscious and willing to gibber. (Nina dauntingly good.) Regarding Jean Tardieu's Unknown Vowel, our quest for, Mr P amusingly points out that we'll only know if we've found it by not being there to know, and there also not being a there either. Much cheering. Mr P wishes us well and leaves.

A 'magnetism' created. No one leaves. By the fourth hour approaching some kind of Protong. Sixth hour – fierce debates in Protong concerning mainly the incredible amount of things which don't exist in our universe compared to the paltry few that do. Ninth/tenth hour, seekers start to go 'through the wall' having blown their own governors (Steve Mattick first contestant through wall, closely followed by one of the Fishes). This wall is not a real wall, it's some blockage in the head. Once you're through it EVERYTHING is funny.

You're aware of the utterly arbitrary nature of everything. Tarmac, cups, ceilings, trees, none of it necessary, ultimate purpose: zero. The whole show from Big Bang to this morning's breakfast all arbitrary battiness, and it's all been far too hot and awful for us to be here up until recently and, as the Universe expands getting colder and colder and too cold for us to be, and on and on winding up as a monstrous ICE monument to its own ludicrousness for having come into being in the first place, the Universe, and while you're outside, beyond the wall, you're OK, you get the joke (see the Bald-Headed Rat), but then a sadness creeps upon you, you are one of the jokes. And began then the most extraordinary antic of laughing (hysterically) with one side of the face and weeping and wailing and gnashing on the other. This kind of thing – (DEMONSTRATION) – and could you laugh and cry AT THE SAME TIME? That became the Quest, can you – (ATTEMPT) – and yes, you can and you go through the middle and, as you go through, in every case, you have a total personal evacuation, stuff out of every orifice, you leave all that old shit behind, but do you feel you've achieved something, are you somewhere, this is deeper than mother, it's other, and as I went through, kerpoo, there was Nina, Nina Plashwit's brilliant four-and-three-quarter-year-old face, brilliant, and I knew that was my commission: TO BE BRILLIANT.

Getting home was interesting because we weren't allowed on the bus. It was late and I crept in at home, but the smell woke my father.

THE BALD-HEADED RAT

Human consciousness dates back to a bald-headed rat-time of the dinosaurs, Plastocene Period. And it's conscious this rat, this bald-headed rat, it knows, and it knows that it knows, and it will evolve several ways: BEAR WOLF PIG LEMUR MONKEY APE US.

As bald-headed rats we wipe out the dinosaurs by scampering up them and pooing in their ears. What consciousness is is a degree of COMPLEXITY and COMPLICATION, sufficient to make the possessor aware that it has IMPORTANCE, PURPOSE and MEANING, but insufficiently complex to work out what this purpose and meaning is IE THAT WE'RE ALL HERE FOR THE ENTERTAINMENT OF DEPRAVED GODS.

But IMPORTANCE prevents us seeing it, IMPORTANCE is the
wall, IMPORTANCE is the spine and structure of the Human Comedy
IMPORTANCE
other side of the wall you get it, other side of the wall you see the
BRILLIANCE of this million-year-long farce, given a glimpse from
the gods, when the gods allowed HUMOUR to trickle in to us
    (HUMOUR came from Africa from the Pygmies due to their lower
viewpoint and the closeness with which they lived with parrots)
it was like them going (!?)
    BUT WE DIDN'T GET IT. TRAPPED in a tragicomic delusion of
his own importance Full-Sized Man discovers fire, invents the Wheel,
Trousers, Tarmac, and the tools and means of utter self-destruction
and awaits only an important enough reason to let them all off.

THE PYGMIES
only the Pygmies who haven't changed for 15,000 (more) years,
whose culture (alone) is one of NON-IMPORTANCE
IMPORTANCE-AVOIDANCE
they know not their age or their birthdays cos why
WHO LAY ON LOONY DANCE SPECTACULARS FOR THE GODS
who evolved from a kindlier, clearer, bald-headed MOUSE line
they never pooed in any dinosaur ears the Pygmies
(or do I sentimentalise? they're dab hands at the Elephant Kill)
        anyway to the Pygmies
        God prosper them

AN OUTBREAK OF MONTANISM
(Summer 1955)
Seagulls suddenly, flocks of them. Neville catches
two seagulls with sardine-baited fishing
lines trailing from a box-kite. Neville's
vivisectional probe into the gulls leads
him to pronounce that seagulls can't fart.
The bore of cheering on the school team.
Off we go, but Neville with big bag of
bread. Doctored bread. Bicarbonate of
soda, possibly, spread on it.
Cricket match. The team fielding. The
seagulls arrive. Neville tossing his bread to them like some
old Doris. Subtle rumble of Protong. Not loud but our lads have heard
it. Then the first of the seagulls detonates in the air, blasts apart into fishy
feather clumps. Boom. Then another. Haha Ahah
(THE LAUGH ON ONE SIDE WEEP ON THE OTHER)
And one of our fielders has an evacuation. Then another ... The more
humorous given the white kit used for cricket.
    There was a big enquiry. Whole school called. Headmaster: grim.
Complains, gentlemen, of an appalling outbreak of Montanism at
Thursday's match. Montanism? Amazing! Was there a word then for
what we'd done? Montanism. Neville hadn't heard of it. We knew what
onanism is. Is Montanism going up a hill to do it? The following now
got banned in our school: the speaking of Pijin or any other voodoo
language (which Pijin isn't). (Voodoo) All ventriloquial studies to cease.

'Sir, will that include Gastromancy?' (PAUSE) Yes. And also banned: speaking in tongues or Glossolalia.

NEVILLE But Sir, Glossolalia can mean that the Holy Ghost is with us. The Headmaster said he'd risk it.

MONTANISM – NEVILLE PLASHWIT (pioneer of ventriloquial therapy) **ADDRESSES THE RADICAL VENTRILOQUISTS** (Kentucky Ventriloquists Convention 1999) Neville recalled the events of the Scout Hut, and the vision he'd got going through the wall was the healing potential of ventriloquism. EG: BEREAVEMENT Loved one dies, regrets, you never said this, shoulda done that, can lead to neurosis. But make a vent doll in which some element of the lost one resides …

EG Walter Lambert and his touching Nurse Lydia Dreams, and the Road Accident Victim vignette. EARLY VENTRILOQUIAL THERAPY The SAMMY doll has got HIS MOTHER'S TEETH IN IT, that mouth is his mother's mouth and Walter, as Nurse Lydia, is his mother's mother.

And now he said he'd like to introduce us to a neglected hero of the gastromantical ventriloquial arts who should be right up there with Bisu the Pygmy (The earliest recorded fool. A comedian, dancer and ventriloquist [gastromancer] later to become the Ancient Egyptian God Bes) THE INCREDIBLE MONTANUS. To get a handle on Montanus we start with data from THE ACTS OF THE APOSTLES after the crucifixion. It's Pentecost time, Jewish Harvest Festival and the Apostles are in rented accommodation in Jerusalem. TONGUES OF FIRE, they say, lick into the place and they find themselves hunting for the lost vowel – BRIEF DEMONSTRATION – and, like happens, they can't stop and they're making such a racket half Jerusalem is drawn to the place to find out what's going on. And some of the 15 identified foreign folk drawn to lurk reckon they're hearing bits and bobs of their own language in the noise, but locals say 'no, they're drunk,' and that's when Peter gets himself together and says, 'no we're not drunk, indeed it is only nine o'clock in the morning. What this is is the New Baptism, and this is the talk of Angels, this is Angels coming through, courtesy of the Holy Spirit, the Holy Ghost you might say.' And, from then on, this antic having been given the fine name of GLOSSOLALIA, or THE GIFT OF TONGUES, everyone, EVERYONE who joins the Church, has to give some kind of showing in the Tongues Department. It's a sign you're in.

And there's a feller who wasn't IN, name of Saul, who thought it was all dangerous bollocks and who wasn't shy of saying so and slinging the odd brick, has a sudden visionary revision on the matter, decides his name's Paul now, and becomes their NUMBER ONE TONGUESTER. We turn now to Corinthians I, chapter 14. The Church of Corinth has written to Paul (Paul's a much older man now with some worries), they've heard he's not so keen on the Glossolalics now. 'The Glossolalics,' sez Paul, 'the Glossolalics, first of all know that I am the main man of THAT. No one has put in as much tongue-time as I.' However, seems to Paul that a lot of the Glossolalia now is recreational, and he's not sure what use it is to the Church UNLESS YOU CAN INTERPRET IT. If people want to do it, have to do it, OK, but only one at a time, two or three at most, not to be encouraged
UNLESS YOU CAN DEVELOP INTERPRETATIVE SKILLS
and what about the women, want to know the Good Men of Corinth?

'Women,' sez Paul, 'women, NO, they mustn't do it, in fact THEY MUSTN'T TALK AT ALL IN CHURCHES. 'Tis foul and a thing of disgustment when women chat in churches. If they've got a query then they must ask their own husbands at home. And that was the Church's stance on the matter until 155 AD.

In a little village in Phrygia, THE PHENOMENAL GASTROMANCER MONTANUS launches his act. MONTANUS a recent convert to Christianity from the Fertility Cult of Cybele and MONTANUS has with him two PriestESSES PRISCA and MAXIMILLA and they are Glossolalic Tonguesters like ne'er before, and they can each interpret for the other, inter-interpret. This is ELVIS AND THE SUPREMES IN SPADES. Whang. Socko. They take the village. Village forms a gastromanting tongueing throng, takes the next village, towns, cities, yea all Phrygia (kinda what we now call Turkey). And interpreted revelations now chuffing up and out, scrolls 'pon scrolls, direct stuff from Angels, Deity, Demons, Fairies. And so it goes for 20 years.

And Montanus sez to the Regular Church: 'Behold I have converted your grim and spotty achievement into ONE JOYOUS EXULTANT FLOCK' and the Church said 'bollocks, they're joyous and exultant for wrong and ridiculous reasons. Their Glossolalicals are recreational and your interpretations are but bogweed.' And they excommunicated Montanus and Prisca and Maximilla, but they couldn't wipe out MontanISM. Church seized the scrolls of Montanic interpretation and burned them, but the fire of Montanism raged on into Africa, Carthage, still going fifth century. Ninth century, a kinda merger of the Great Heretic Movements:

The MONTANISTS, aka the CATAPHRYGIANS, THE BOOGERS, THE KATARS, THE ESSENES, THE ARIANS ('Different stuff!'), THE FOLLOWERS OF THE FISH AND THE WINKING EYE, THE NOSTICS WITH A SILENT G, THE Gs WITH A SILENT NOSTIC, THE BOYS AND GIRLS OF THE LAUGHING JESUS, THE GENTLEMEN OF THE HOOTING BUDDHA, THE FAT POTTERS, THE HOLY JUGS, THE NAUGHTY BOYS, THE BRETHEN AND SISTEREN OF THE FREE SPIRIT, PIRATES OF THE SHATTERED MIRROR, THE CHILDREN OF BISU

Dolly Parton
Dolly Parton was in the audience, or some dame who looked just like Dolly Parton and she looked at me, Dolly Parton did, and blew me a kiss,
Dolly Parton

Neville continuing: NOT COMEDY routines then, but ECSTASY and HILARITY routines performed in a gross-out/twitch/jerk/body-explosive language, megajoyful, megaPAINFUL, through the wall, ultimate AND BEYOND VOCABULARY'S RESTRAINT.

These are the folk of whom Rabelais wrote, these FULL-ON/FULL-OUT, anything comes/everything goes extravaganzas are profoundly affecting RELAXATIVES, and can only be performed in Mead Hall BATHhouses where you can hose away quantities of orificular evacuative PLUSH SEATING IS THE FINAL NAIL IN THE COFFIN OF REAL COMEDY

But GOD had a word with the POPE, and the POPE had a word with the GENERALS: the sin of being happy for wrong and ridiculous reasons. You're not meant to be happy HERE. HEAVEN'S for being happy in (the last bonfires of that round of the Inquisition: 1256). AUDIENCES ENTERTAINERS SCRIPTS PROPS SCENERY and VENUES – all was burned

And yet MONTANISM, under other names, arising seemingly self-ignited from the ashes. THE JANSENIST CONVULSIONARIES, THE

CAMISARDS (a bunch of seventeenth-century gastromancers slung out of France for chuffing up the dead, and recreational glossolalia likened to the roaring of tuskered sea denizens, at whose London gatherings alchemist and Arien ('different stuff!') Sir Isaac Newton frolicked with his Swiss boyfriend, Fatio de Duillier), the early QUAKERS, the SHAKERS, the JERKERS, us in the Anal Forest Sea Scout Hut but, more to the point, THE PENTECOSTAL CHURCH (see also THE CHARISMATICS, THE HOLY GHOSTERS, THE TORONTO BLESSING, THE CHURCH OF ELVIS).

PENTACOSTALISM: US, circa 1900. The Pentecostals who are MONTANISM RAMPANT, 15 million members now and growing. The Pentecostals, who give work to the vent, 15 million going through the wall on a weekly basis. NIGHTLY some.

After a successful ventriloquial recovery Neville steers his patients, he tells us, into the vital recuperative THRU THE WALL PROGRAM offered by the PENTECOSTAL CHURCH

'Fellow Radical Vents I urge an addition to our Honours Board, the names of PRISCA, MAXIMILLA and, obviously, himself, MONTANUS OF PHRYGIA. Thank you.'

Whooping

Dolly Parton hands up some art work she's done, Montanus in period jockstrap and feathers. Prisca and Maximilla, science-fantasy heroines. The three of them fiendishly, deliciously tonguing, the while chuff-inhaling the wilder characters of Hieronymous Bosch, amongst whom the rat, the bald-headed rat, who knows that he knows that he knows.

Neville strutting humbly. I wonder what his knob looked like now with all these years of desiccated mouse in it.

Lovely Dolly Parton's lovely tits ❑

From Ken Campbell's History of Comedy. Part One: Ventriloquism, *which played at the Royal National Theatre, London from 25 August to 7 September 2000. His plays are published by Methuen.* © *Ken Campbell. Credit for all illustrations: Vladimir Seledtsov*

The wit and wisdom of Pitkin

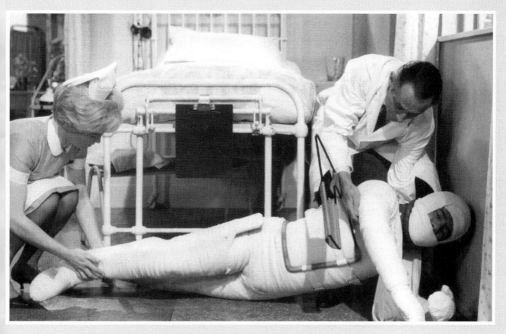

Norman Wisdom in A Stitch in Time. *Credit: Courtesy of Carlton International Media Ltd*

Through years of ideological isolation, British comedian Norman Wisdom lighted the gloom of Enver Hoxha's Albania, articulating out loud what his cowed subjects dared not whisper. Foreign films were one of the country's only windows on the outside world. The comedies of Norman Wisdom, known as Pitkin, were by far the most successful.

After 1973, even these were banned, condemned as 'foreign manifestations … with a negative influence on the spiritual tranquillity and peace of mind of the Albanian people'. However, after a decade of nothing but the products of the *Shqipëria e re* (New Albania) film studio, foreign films began to creep back.

Though Wisdom had been out of fashion for decades in the UK, the news that Pitkin would be screened every Sunday after the 8.30pm news bulletin was the major event of 1982. Even the censors kept quiet. The entire Wisdom oeuvre was screened again in 1987. It took dramatic political change and a further decade, but Albanians did finally have the last laugh on Hoxha when Wisdom came to Tirana and finally met his keenest fans. ❑

Mira Blushi is director of international relations at Albanian Radio and TV

MOHAMED FELLAG

The case of the dead elephant

'Laughing where it hurts. That's my way of combating the evils which eat away at my country: poverty, censorship, taboos, intolerance, machismo, hatred of love, fatalism ... Making people laugh every evening is an extreme act of resistance'

Censorship? It's ruined the telly in Algeria! Like it says in the ads: 'ALGERIAN NATIONAL TELEVISION is the programme that keeps YOU programmed!'

There are three kinds of censorship in Algerian TV: political censorship, moral censorship and self-censorship. Political censorship? That's easy: every time there's anything serious happening on the political front, what do they put on the telly? Animal programmes, that's what! So, seeing there's quite often something serious happening on the political front, Jacques-Yves Cousteau has become a really big star!

When we had the popular uprising on 5 October 1988, it was *RATATATATAT* in the streets, Kalashnikovs all day long, 600 dead, HELP! I WANT ME MUM! And people dashed to the telly to get the news, and what was on the whole day? 'The Plankton-eating Fish of the Deep Oceans'. In Algeria, we're all experts on plankton now!

But your Algerian's a clever bloke, oh yes; he's got it sussed! He's worked out how to decipher these animal programmes. I remember once, back in the late 1970s, they were showing a documentary about a herd of elephants. Right, so there they are, on the savannah, chomping the grass and, suddenly, one of them goes off on his own, away from the herd, and heads for the elephants' graveyard. He drops to his knees, rolls over, and he's dead. Next morning, on the streets in Algiers, the word is: 'Hey, listen, mate, have you heard? Boumedienne's dead [President of

Algeria 1965–78]. Yeah, really, I saw it on the news.' Algerian television is the only television in the world where they use real animals on the *Bébête Show* [satirical French comedy in which politicians were represented as animals].

But the kind of censorship that's caused most problems is moral censorship. And its biggest victim is the screen kiss. Mind you, they don't cut out all kisses; well, at least they didn't until 1987–88. They only cut out kisses between irregular partners. Unmarried couples: no kissing! But maybe if there's a film actor and he's not married to her at the beginning of the film, but early on in the film he promises the young actress he's going to marry her by the time the film finishes …Well, OK

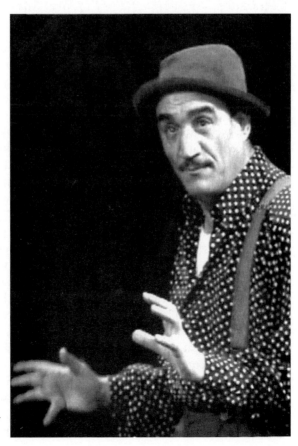

Mohamed Fellag in his show Djurdjurassique Bled, *1999. Credit: Courtesy of Passion Pilote*

then, but only if you do marry her. No changing the plot, right? OK, if you marry her, you can go ahead and give her a kiss, but just a little one mind, none of your tonsil-polishing jobs!

So when they cut out all the kissing, it completely wrecks the film; it doesn't make sense any more. We can't follow what's going on. You see the actor heading towards the actress and then, when they're just getting to the point where ... PING ... the film jumps and we're all saying, 'Hey, what happened there, then? The bloke been eating garlic or something?' And if you see a character who isn't married kissing an actress at the beginning of the film, you can tell straight away that he's going to marry her at the end. 'Right, OK, got it, know what's gonna happen, they've given the game away, it's that sort of film.'

And it's like that with *Dallas*. In Algeria, what they've done with *Dallas*, they've taken all the kissing out, got rid of all the one-to-one scenes with a man and a woman, all the swimming pool bits, all that. So what's left? All the characters in *Dallas* do nothing but work! They just stick to working hours! So, like JR, for example: you see him working, working, everything's going along fine. He's supposed to be meeting SueEllen at six o'clock – they don't show you that, but you know about it. Right, well, quarter to six, he stands up, puts his jacket on, sets off to meet Sue Ellen and ... Hi there! There he is, back at work again! Sometimes you see the young male lead driving along in his open-top sports car. Here we go, everything's great ... brrrm, brrrm ... due to meet his girlfriend at eight o'clock, and she'll be wearing next to nothing (they don't show you that, but we know, we know!). Here he comes, 100mph, screeches to a halt, jumps out of the car; he's so keen he runs up 18 flights of stairs. Gets to the top, rings the bell, DING, DONG. Right, so in Algeria, the censor, the guy with the scissors, what does he do? There's the door of the girlfriend's apartment. So he looks through the rest of the episode until he finds another door, AND HE STICKS IT IN HERE! So, when the bloke who's coming to see his girlfriend opens the door, 'Oh, yes, yes, come on, come on, yeaaaah ...' Here he is, back at the office again! In Algeria, I'll tell you what *Dallas* is, it's a documentary on office life in the USA.

So how is it actually done? Well, there's an office for television censorship, the telly itself and the censor with his scissors. And they say to him: 'Pay attention; be very, very careful. YOU ARE THE KEEPER WHO STANDS AT THE GATES OF MORALITY! Be very careful that not a single kiss gets past if it threatens to destabilise the whole of society. Be especially careful, ESPECIALLY CAREFUL about FRENCH films. Oh, they are a problem, those French films! The amount of work they give us, it's enough to drive you potty! They do nothing in their films except eat and kiss. Sometimes they don't even bother to eat! There are gonna be times when, if you've got a French film, you might just have to show the credits and throw the film itself away. A couple of pounds of food, one actor, one actress, the French, they've got a film! That's all it takes! So, the minute you see an actor and an actress sitting down to eat in a French film, watch out – even if it's his mother, don't trust it, you never know with these infidels.

When they're getting to the dessert stage, that's when you've got to be ready. If he picks up a cherry, puts it in his mouth and tries to push it into his girlfriend's mouth, SNIP. SNIP, SNIP! But keep the cherry, so we can put all the bits of cherry together and make a nice typically Algerian-style film about cherries.

And if you see a couple walking along the road, OK, right, fine, no problem, just walking along the road in Paris or New York, and then suddenly they turn off into a side street and disappear behind a building so you can't see them any more. WHAT ARE THEY DOING BEHIND THE BUILDING? There's plenty of room, what do they have to go behind a building for? So if you're suspicious that they might be up to something, then 30 million Algerians are going to be suspicious about it as well – some of them are even going to get up and have a look behind the telly. So if you're suspicious – get rid of the building, get rid of the whole district if you have to! ❏

Fellag, who now lives in Paris, is currently touring France with his show, A Boat to Australia. *His CD* Djurdjurassique Bled *(1999) is available through Mélodie Distribution. Translated by Mike Routledge*

PIETER-DIRK UYS

On the good ship rainbow nation

South Africa's leading comedian explains that freeedom does not always lend enchantment

In the middle of the year 2000, the biggest news in South Africa is a commission of inquiry into match-fixing by the Springbok cricket captain Hansie Cronje. The revelation that this white Afrikaner hero had cheated at a game sent vibrations of horror through the 40 million people who care. You think that? Not really. Most of the people in this country don't read the newspapers. Many because they still can't read; others because they can't afford a newspaper; and the rest because they know the newspapers are aimed at a certain minority in the country – those who have money. In other words, whites. Which brings me back to the crooked cricket captain. The daily reporting of corruption, theft, murder, fraud and worse, among blacks, is often shrugged off as expected by the whites, while misdemeanours by a white are acknowledged with horror.

It has been six years since Nelson Mandela became the first democratically elected president. Remembering that he had spent 27 years in prison for his beliefs, he could have said: 'Occupy the farms; kill the whites!', and the world would have looked the other way, because we whites had to pay for what we had done. You think that? No, we were forgiven. Mandela took us by the hand and, in Afrikaans, asked us to walk with him on that path to freedom.

Love your enemy – it will ruin his reputation!

He was sworn in at the Union Building in Pretoria. He could have had the ceremony in Soweto, or on Robben Island, but he chose to herald the rebirth of South Africa on the spot where, in 1966, they buried the assassinated architect of apartheid, Hendrik Verwoerd.

That shows a great sense of humour.

In 1994, South Africa was on everyone's lips and T-shirts. Souvenirs of the Berlin Wall took pride of place next to pictures of Mandela and the queues of millions of South Africans waiting in the African sun for days to vote.

The magic is over.

The Berlin Wall stone is somewhere in the garden, lost among other stones that never divided nations. Nelson Mandela on T-shirts just shows a lack of fashion because the T-shirts are old.

Thabo Mbeki does not appear on T-shirts. The new president is seldom seen on TV. In fact, one wonders if he's not just a virtual leader. Even the address of what should have been his web page, www.thabombeki.com, has been hijacked by cybersquatters in the USA!

WHITES WHO NEVER BENEFITTED FROM APARTHEID:

ZAPIRO

We see more of Thabo Mbeki at Bill Clinton's side or talking
to Chancellor Schroeder and Tony Blair, and shaking hands and
exchanging smiles with Robert Mugabe of Zimbabwe. The newspapers
scream: 'Condemn Mugabe for his overt racism!', but Mbeki does it his
way. Quiet diplomacy or, to put it bluntly: not in the racist headlines of
the local media! President Mbeki is not trying to fill Nelson Mandela's
footsteps. He, and everyone else, would disappear. No one can fill
Mandela's shadow. But Mbeki is an astute African politician with a
gentle European style. He is patient and original. We've had the world
statesman; we now need the organiser, the manager, the chief executive
officer. You believe this? Not any more. Suddenly, in the face of 99% of
the world accepting that HIV leads to AIDS, President Mbeki surfs the
Internet, discovers aliens and the Illuminati, and proclaims that AIDS
comes from Venus, while HIV comes from Mars.

So while on the bridge of this new liner called Rainbow Nation, a
confused and careless cabal of politicians organises itself with 15% salary
increases, education is trying to catch up with 360 years of propaganda
and elitism. Health is marginalised by the plague of AIDS, not made
simpler by urban legends that convince men with the disease to find a
cure by raping a child. Fatal mistakes are being made and then ignored.
Forty million free condoms are released into our society, each condom
carefully stapled to a card explaining why they should be used. The
promise of one million houses in five years was on the optimistic side,
but most South Africans now have electricity and water. This is one of
the most important things to have happened here since 1994. Granted,
we all have the vote now. We all have the protection of a constitution
and a Bill of Rights. And Mrs Winnie Madikizela-Mandela is not yet
president! All good news! And for the first time, the majority can switch
on a light and run a bath!

The triumph of Mandela's reconciliation has been the peaceful
transition from apartheid to democracy. Violence is still the issue of the
day, with murder and rape placing our country in the world's top five.
But remember: there were three armies trained and ready to fight a civil
war, and the war was cancelled.

There was much hatred and anger – there still is. But there are also
hopes and dreams and the luxury of complaints. It's a very successful
democracy because everyone is equally dissatisfied!

Last year, before the second election on 2 June, we undertook a voter-education-through-entertainment tour of the country. Travelling 10,000 kilometres through nine provinces, presenting 60 free shows in townships and cities, in community centres and school halls, using my most famous character, Mrs Evita Bezuidenhout, to entertain people with the reality of what democracy is: that the vote is secret and sacred; to make a cross on your ballot, not a tick; that all citizens have the right to decide; to celebrate our democracy by protecting freedom with education.

Ninety per cent of our audiences were black – as they should be – for this is a big black country with a small white lining. The extraordinary sense of humour from the people, their calm patience and positive attitude to the future, cancelled out the negative whingeing and complaining round the dinner tables of finance and the headlines of commerce. The people are still excited and willing to take a chance together, in spite of the fears and the horrors of violence, poverty, disease and joblessness.

During a performance for 1,000 young blacks, enjoying their entertainment, asking questions of Mrs Evita Bezuidenhout, this Afrikaner 'woman' who doesn't even exist, a young 18-year-old man stood up. He was going to vote for the first time. He was passionate about his love for his country. He was energetic in his confidence. He was angry! He said it all.

'We fought for freedom! All we got was democracy!' ❏

Pieter-Dirk Uys *is South Africa's leading comedian*

BILL HICKS

Dear Bill

O n 1 October 1994, the comedian Bill Hicks, after doing his twelfth gig on the David Letterman show, became the first comedy act to be censored at CBS's Ed Sullivan Theatre, where Letterman was in residence and where Elvis Presley was famously censored in 1956. Presley was not allowed to be shown from the waist down. Hicks was not allowed to be shown at all. It's not what was in Hicks' pants but what was in his head that scared the CBS panjandrums.

Hicks, a tall 31-year-old Texan with a podgy face, aged beyond its years from hard living on the road, was no motormouth vulgarian but an exhilarating comic thinker in a renegade class all his own. Until the ban, which, according to Hicks, earned him 'more attention than my other 11 appearances on Letterman times 100', Hicks' caustic observations and mischievous cultural connections had found a wide audience in the UK, where he is still something of a cult figure.

Hicks certainly went for broke and pronounced his real comic self in the banned Letterman performance, which he wrote out for me in a 39-page letter that also recounts his version of events. Hicks had to write out his set because the tape of it, which the Letterman people said they'd send three weeks earlier, had not yet reached him. Hicks, who delivered his monologue dressed not in his usual gunslinger black but in 'bright fall colours, an outfit bought just for the show and reflective of my bright and cheerful mood', seemed to have a lot to smile about. Letterman, who Hicks says greeted him as he sat down to talk with, 'Good set, Bill! Always nice to have you drop by with an uplifting message!' and signed off saying, 'Bill, enjoy answering your mail for the next few weeks,' had been seen to laugh. The word in the green room was also good. A couple of hours later, Hicks was back in his hotel, wearing nothing but a towel, when the call came from Robert Morton, the executive producer of the Letterman show, telling him he'd been deep-sixed. Hicks sat down on the bed.

John Lahr, The New Yorker, 1 November 1994

What follows is an edited version of Hicks' hitherto unpublished letter.

Dear John,

Here is the material (verbatim) that CBS's standards and practices found 'unsuitable' for the viewing public in 1993, year of our Lord. These are the 'hotspots' I believe were not mentioned. I'm going to include audience responses as well, for it does play a part in my thoughts on the incident which will follow the jokes. Jokes, John: this is what America now fears – one man with a point of view, speaking out, unafraid of our vaunted institutions, or the loathsome superstitions the CBS hierarchy feels the masses (the herd) use as their religion.

I'm feeling good. The set I've prepared has been approved and reapproved by Mary Connelly, the segment producer of the show. It is exactly the same set that was approved for the previous Friday, the night where I was 'bumped' due to lack of time. It is the material that I am excited about performing, for it best reflects – out of all the other appearances I've made on the show – myself.

BILL Good evening! I'm very excited to be here tonight, and I'm very excited because I got some great news today. I've finally got my own TV show coming out as a replacement show this fall!
The audience applauds.
BILL Don't worry, it's not a talk show.
The audience laughs.
BILL Thank God! It's a half-hour weekly show that I will be hosting, entitled 'Let's Hunt and Kill Billy Ray Cyrus'.
Audience bursts into laughter and applause.
BILL I think it's fairly self-explanatory. Each week we let the Hounds of Hell loose and chase the jar-head, no talent, cracker-idiot all over the globe till I finally catch that fruity little ponytail of his, pull him to his chippendale's knees, put a shotgun in his mouth and 'pow'.
Audience continues to applaud and laugh.
BILL Then we'll be back in '94 with 'Let's Hunt and Kill Michael Bolton'.
Audience laughs and applauds.
BILL Yeah, so you can see that, with guests like this, our run will be fairly limitless.
Audience laughs.
BILL And we're kicking the whole series off with our MC Hammer,

Credit: Courtesy Strauss-Mcgarr Entertainment

Vanilla Ice, Markie Mark Christmas special ...
Audience laughs and applauds.
BILL And I don't want to give any surprises away, but the first one we
hunt and kill on that show is Markie Mark, because his pants keep falling
around his ankles and he can't run away ...
Bill mimes a hobbling Markie Mark. The audience laughs.
BILL Yeah, I get to cross-bow him right in the abs. It's a beautiful thing.
Bring the family. Tape it. It's definitely a show for the nineties ...
Audience applauds.

At this point I did a line about men dancing. Since it was never
mentioned as a reason for excising me from the show, let's skip ahead to
the next 'hot point' that *was* mentioned (by the way, the joke about men
dancing got a huge laugh).

BILL You know, I consider myself an open-minded person. But speaking of homosexuality, something has come to my attention that has shocked even me, Have you heard about these new grade school books for children they're trying to add to the curriculum, to help children understand the gay lifestyle. One's called *Heather's Two Mommies* and the other is called *Daddy's New Roommate*.

Here I make a shocked, disgusted, face.

BILL Folks, I gotta draw the line here and say this is absolutely disgusting. It is grotesque, and it is pure evil.

Pause.

BILL I'm talking, of course, about *Daddy's New Roommate*.

Audience laughs.

BILL *Heather's Two Mommies* is quite fetching. You know they're hugging on page seven.

Audience laughs.

BILL (*lasciviously*) Ooh! Go Mommies, go! Ooh! They kiss in chapter four!

Audience laughs.

BILL Me and my nephew wrestle over that book every night ...

Bill mimes his little nephew jumping up and down.

BILL (*as nephew*) Uncle Bill, I've gotta do my homework.

Audience laughs.

BILL Shut up and do your math! I'm proof-reading this for you ...

Audience laughs.

We move directly into the next 'hot point'.

BILL You know who's really bugging me these days. These pro-lifers ...

Smattering of applause.

BILL You ever look at their faces? 'I'm pro-life!'

Bill makes a pinched face of hate and fear, his lips are pursed as though he's just sucked on a lemon.

BILL 'I'm pro-life!' Boy, they look it don't they? They just exude *joie de vie*. You just want to hang with them and play Trivial Pursuit all night long.

Audience chuckles.

BILL You know what bugs me about them? If you're so pro-life, do me a favour – don't lock arms and block medical clinics. If you're so pro-life, lock arms and block cemeteries.

Audience laughs.
BILL Let's see how committed you are to this idea.
Bill mimes the pursed lipped pro-lifers locking arms.
BILL (*as pro-lifer*) She can't come in!
Audience laughs.
BILL (*as confused member of funeral procession*) She was 98. She was hit by a bus!
Audience laughs.
BILL (*as pro-lifer*) There's options!
Audience laughs.
BILL (*as confused member of funeral procession*) What else can we do? Have her stuffed?
Audience laughs.
BILL I want to see pro-lifers with crowbars at funerals opening caskets – 'get out!' Then I'd be really impressed by their mission.
Audience laughs and applauds.

At this point I did a routine on smoking, which was never brought up as a 'hot point', so let's move ahead to the end of my routine, and another series of jokes that were mentioned as 'unsuitable'.

BILL I've been travelling a lot lately. I was over in Australia during Easter. It was interesting to note that they celebrate Easter the same way as we do – commemorating the death and resurrection of Jesus by telling our children a giant bunny rabbit left chocolate eggs in the night.
Audience laughs.
BILL I wonder why we're so messed up as a race? You know, I've read the Bible – can't find the words 'bunny' or 'chocolate' in the whole book.
Audience laughs.
BILL Where do we get this stuff from? And why those two things? Why not 'goldfish left Lincoln logs in our sock drawers'? I mean, as long as we are making things up, why not go hog wild?
Audience laughs and applauds.
BILL I think it's interesting how people act on their beliefs. A lot of Christians, for instance, wear crosses around their necks. Nice sentiment, but do you think that when Jesus comes back, he's really going to want to look at a cross?

Audience laughs. Bill makes a face of pain and horror.
BILL Ow. Maybe that's why he hasn't shown up yet ...
Audience laughs.
BILL (*as Jesus looking down from heaven*) I'm not going, Dad, no, they're
still wearing crosses – they totally missed the point. When they start
wearing fishes, I might go back again ... no, I'm not going ... OK, I'll
tell you what – I'll go back as a bunny ...
Audience bursts into applause and laughter. The band kicks into Revolution
by The Beatles.
BILL Thank you very much! Good night!
Bill crosses over to the seat next to Letterman's desk.
LETTERMAN Good set, Bill! Always nice to have you drop by with an
uplifting message!
Audience and Bill laugh. Cut to commercial.

Then closes the show with ...

LETTERMAN I want to thank our guests tonight – Andie McDowell,
Graham Parker, and Bill Hicks ... Bill, enjoy answering your mail over
the next few weeks. Goodnight everybody!
The audience and Bill crack up at Letterman's closing line.

... and we're off the air.

Bill Sheft, a comic and one of the writers on the show, comes up to
me saying, 'Hicks, that was great!' I ask him if he thinks Letterman
liked it. Bill Sheft, whose other duties include warming up the audience
and getting them to applaud when the show goes in and out of
commercials says, 'Are you kidding? Letterman was cracking up
throughout the whole set.'
   Since I am a fan of Dave's and the show, it meant a lot to me that
he enjoyed my work. The fact that it was over, and by *all* accounts went
fine, was a huge relief.
   After the show, I returned to my hotel and took a long hot bath. As
I was getting out of the tub, the phone rang. It was now half past seven.
Robert Morton, the producer of the Letterman show, was on the line.
He said, 'Bill, I've got some bad news ...' My first thought was that Dave
had been chopped up and sautéed by the mob cook. Robert Morton

went on, 'Bill, we've had to edit your set from tonight's show.'

I sat down on the bed, stunned, wearing nothing but a towel. 'I don't understand, Robert. What's the problem? I thought the show went great.'

Morton replied, 'It did, Bill. You killed out there. It's just that the CBS Standards and Practices felt that some of the material was unsuitable for broadcast.'

I rubbed my head, confused. 'Ah. Which material did they find unsuitable?'

'Well,' Morty replied, 'almost all of it. If I had to edit everything they object to, there'd be nothing left of the set, so we just think it's best to cut you entirely from the show. Bill, we fought tooth and nail to keep the set as it is, but Standards and Practices won't back down and David is furious. We're all upset here. What can I say? It's out of my hands now. We've never experienced this before with Standards and Practices, and they're just not going to back down. I'm really sorry.'

'But, Bob, they're so obviously jokes ...'

'Bill, I know, I know. But Standards and Practices just doesn't find them suitable.'

'But which ones? I mean, I ran this set by my 63-year-old Mom on her porch in Little Rock, Arkansas. You're not going to find *anyone* more mainstream, nor any place more Middle America, than my Mom in Little Rock, Arkansas, and she had no problem with the material.'

'Bill, what can I say? It's out of our hands, Bill. We'll just try and schedule a different set in a couple of weeks and have you back on.'

Then Morton said, 'Bill, we take full responsibility for this. It's our fault. We should have spent more time before working on the set, so Mary and I could have edited out the "hot points", and we wouldn't be having to do this now.'

Finally, I came to my senses. I said, 'Bob, they're just jokes. I don't want them to be edited by you. Why are people so afraid of jokes?'

To this, Morty replied, 'Bill, you have to understand our audiences.'

This is a line I've heard before and it always pisses me off. 'Your audiences!' I retorted, 'what? Do you grow them on farms? Your audience is comprised of "people", right? Well, I understand people, being a person myself. People are who I play to every night, Bob, and we get along just fine ... And when I'm not performing on your show, *I'm* a member of the audience for your show. Are you saying that my material is not suitable for *me*? This doesn't make sense. Why do you underestimate the intelligence of the audience? I think that shows a great deal of contempt on your part ...'

Morty bursts in with, 'Bill, it's not our decision. We have to answer to the networks, and this is the way they want to handle it. Again, I'm sorry – you're not at fault here. Now let me get to work on editing you from the show and we'll set another date as soon as possible with some different material, OK?'

'What kind of material? How bad airline food is? Boy, 7-11s sure are expensive? Golly, Ross Perot has big ears? Bob, you keep saying that you want me on the show, then you don't let me be myself, and now you're cutting me out completely. I feel like a beaten wife who keeps coming back for more. I try and write the best material I can for you guys. Yours is the only show I do because I'm a big fan, and I think you're the best talk show on television. And this is how you treat me?'

'Bill, that's just the way it is sometimes. I'm sorry, OK.'

'Well, I'm sorry, too, Bob. Now I've got to call my folks back and tell them not to wait up. I've got to call all my friends ...'

'Bill, I know. This is tough on all of us.'

'Well, you've got to do what you've got to do ... OK.' Then we hang up.

So there you have it. Not since Elvis was censored from the waist down has a performer, a comic, performing on the very same stage, been so censored – now from the neck up – in America. For telling jokes.

'What are they so afraid of?' I yelled. 'Goddamnit! I'm a fan of the show. I'm an audience member. I do my best shit for them ... they're just jokes.' Here's this show I loved, that touted itself as this hip late-night talk show, trying to silence one man's voice, a comic, no less.

Apparently, many of my media friends, fans and supporters are also Letterman fans. They felt that this was a story that was newsworthy and expressed to me their own sympathy and outrage over what had occurred. Thursday came and went and still no tape arrived, so I took it upon myself to call Robert Morton personally. I asked why the tape hadn't arrived yet, and he said, 'Um. I don't know if we are legally allowed to send out a tape of an unaired segment of a show.'

I thought this had just come off the top of his head so I said, 'Robert, I just want it for my archives, and my parents would love to see it,' to which Morty replied, 'I understand. I'll get you the tape. And let's work on another set for a few weeks from now.'

'Great,' I said, and hung up. To this day, no tape has ever arrived.

Since there was so much interest from the media, we decided to go ahead and do some interviews. One radio talk show I did, the *Alan Bennet Show* in San Francisco, had a live studio audience the morning I called in to be interviewed. The studio audience laughed at the jokes as I told them, and applauded the points I made about television after hearing the jokes. One person who heard the broadcast took it upon himself to write a stinging letter to CBS, chastising them for their cowardice for not airing my set. He quickly received a letter in reply which was then forwarded to my office. Its contents were most interesting and added a humorous twist to the already black comedy that was unfolding. I have CBS's reply before me, and quote: '... it is true that Bill Hicks was taped that evening and that his performance did not air. What is inaccurate is that the deletion of his routine was required by CBS. In fact, although a CBS Programme Practices editor works on the show, the decision was *solely that of the producers* of the programme with that of another comedian. Therefore, your criticism that CBS censored the programme is *totally without foundation*. Creative judgement must be made in the course of producing any programme, and, while we regret that you disagreed with this one, the producers thought it necessary, and this is a decision we would not override.'

I did what I've always done – performed material in a comedic way, which I thought was funny. The artist always plays to himself, and I believe the audience, seeing that one person can be free to express his thoughts, however strange they may seem, inspires the audience to feel that perhaps they too can freely express their innermost thoughts with impunity, joy and release, and perhaps discover our common bond – unique, yet so similar – with each other. This philosophy may appear at first to some as selfish – 'I play to me and do material that interests and cracks me up.' But, you see, I don't feel I'm different from anyone else. The audience *is* me. I believe we all have the same voice of reason inside us, and that voice is the same in everyone.

This is what I think CBS, the producers of the Letterman show, the networks and governments fear the most – that one man free, expressing his own thoughts and point of view, might somehow inspire others to think for themselves and listen to that voice of reason inside them, and then perhaps, one by one we will awaken from this dream of lies and illusions that the world, the governments and their propaganda arm, the mainstream media, feeds us continuously over fifty-two channels, twenty-four hours a day. What I realised was that they don't want the people to be awake. The elite ruling class wants us asleep so we'll remain a docile, apathetic herd of passive consumers and non-participants in the true agendas of our governments, which is to keep us separate and present an image of a world filled with unresolvable problems, that they, and only they, might somewhere, in the never-arriving future, may be able to solve. Just stay asleep, America. Keep watching television. Keep paying attention to the infinite witnesses of illusion we provide you over 'Lucifer's Dream Box'.

The herd has been pacified by our charade of concern as we pose the two most idiotic questions imaginable – 'Is television becoming too violent?' and 'Is television becoming too promiscuous?' The answer, my friends, is this: television is too stupid. It treats us like morons. Case closed.

And now, the final irony. One of the 'hot points' that was brought up as being 'unsuitable for our audience' was my joke about pro-lifers. My brilliant friend Andy posited the theory that this was really what bothered and scared the network the most, seeing as how the 'pro-life' movement has essentially become a terrorist group acting with impunity and God on their side, in a country where the reasonable majority overwhelmingly supports freedom of choice regarding abortion. I felt there was something to this theory, but I was still surprised to be watching the Letterman Show (I'm still a fan) the Monday night following my censored Friday night performance and, lo and behold, they cut to a – are you ready for this? – pro-life commercial. This farce is now complete. 'Follow the money!'

Then I'll see you all in heaven, where we can really share a great laugh together

... Forever and ever and ever. With love, Bill Hicks. ❏

John Lahr *is a writer based in London and New York. He is the author of* Light Fantastic: Adventures in Theatre *(Bloomsbury) and* Prick Up Your Ears: The Biography of Joe Orton *(Penguin)*

PAUL KRASSNER

The busting of Lenny

Lenny was in mock shock. 'Do you realise,' he asked rhetorically, 'that they're busting kids for smoking flowers?' But Lenny was an optimist. It was in 1960 that he said, 'Now let me tell you something about pot. Pot will be legal in ten years. Why? Because in this audience, probably every other one of you knows a law student who smokes pot, who will become a senator, who will legalise it to protect himself.'

A sense of optimism was the essence of Lenny Bruce's humour, especially at its most controversial. And so, when it was discovered that Nazi leaders from Germany had resettled in Argentina with false passports, he displayed from the stage a newspaper with a huge headline: 'Six Million Jews Found Alive in Argentina!' Now, that was the ultimate extension of optimism.

Lenny poked fun at the ridiculously high fees in show business by comparing them with the absurdly low salaries of teachers. He explored the implications of pornography, masturbation and orgasms before they were trendy subjects and became the basis of a US$8bn industry.

He ventured into fields that were mined with taboos, breaking from a long tradition of mainstream stand-up comics who remained loyal to safe material. They spewed forth a bland plethora of stereotypical jokes about mothers-in-law, Chinese waiters, women drivers, Marilyn Monroe, airplane food, Elvis Presley and the ever popular complaints about 'my wife', whether it had to do with her cooking, her shopping, her nagging or her frigidity.

I first met Lenny in 1959 when he came to New York for a midnight show at Town Hall. He was a charter subscriber to my satirical magazine,

The Realist, and he invited me to his hotel, where he was staying with
Eric Miller, a black musician who worked with Lenny in certain bits,
such as 'How to Relax Coloured People at a Party'. Lenny would
portray a 'first-plateau liberal' trying to make conversation with Miller,
playing the part of an entertainer at an all-white party.

Lenny's satire was his way of responding to a culture wallowing
in its own hypocrisy. If it was considered sick to have a photo of him
picnicking in a cemetery on the cover of his first album, he knew it was
really sicker to enforce racial segregation of the bodies that were allowed
to be buried in that cemetery.

At this point in his career, Lenny was still using the euphemism 'frig'
on stage. Although the mainstream media were already translating his
irreverence into 'sick comic', he had not yet been branded 'filthy'. I
handed him the new issue of *The Realist* featuring my interview with
psychotherapist Albert Ellis, which included a segment on the semantics
of profanity.

'My premise,' said Dr Ellis, 'is that sexual intercourse, copulation,
fucking or whatever you wish to call it, is normally, under almost all
circumstances, a damned good thing. Therefore, we should rarely use it
in a negative, condemnatory manner. Instead of denouncing someone
by calling him "a fucking bastard", we should say, of course, that he is
"an unfucking villain" (since bastard, too, is not necessarily a negative
state and should not only be used pejoratively).'

Lenny was amazed that I could get away with publishing that without
resorting to asterisks or dashes as other magazines did then.

'Are you telling me that this is legal to sell on the newsstands?'

'Absolutely,' I said. 'The Supreme Court's definition of obscenity
is that it has to be material which appeals to your prurient interest ...'

Lenny magically produced an unabridged dictionary from the suitcase
on his bed, and he proceeded to look up the word prurient, which has
its roots in the Latin *prurie* – to itch.

'To itch,' he mused. 'What does that mean? That they can bust a
novelty-store owner for selling itching powder along with the dribble
glass and the whoopee cushion?'

'It's just their way of saying that something gets you horny.'

He closed the dictionary, clenching his jaw and nodding his head
in affirmation of a new discovery: 'So it's against the law to get you
horny ...'

PAUL KRASSNER

In September 1961, Lenny was arrested, ostensibly for drugs (for which he had a prescription), but actually because he was making too much money and local officials wanted a piece of the action. He was appearing at the Red Hill Inn in Pennsauken, New Jersey, near Philadelphia. Cops broke into his hotel room to make the arrest, and that night an attorney and bail bondsman came backstage and told him that US$10,000 was all it would take for the judge to dismiss the charges. Lenny refused. A lawyer friend happened to witness this attempted extortion; the others assumed he was a beatnik just hanging around the dressing room. That was on Friday. On Monday, Lenny went to court and pleaded not guilty. 'Incidentally,' he added, 'I can only come up with US$50.' The case was dismissed.

Five days later, at the Jazz Workshop in San Francisco, Lenny was arrested for portraying a Broadway agent who used the word 'cocksucker' to describe a drag queen. This was the first in a series of arrests, ostensibly for obscenity, but actually for choosing religious and political icons as targets in his stream-of-consciousness performances.

Lenny was writing an autobiography, *How to Talk Dirty and Influence People*, which *Playboy* magazine planned to serialise then publish as a book, and they hired me as his editor. We hooked up in Atlantic City, where Lenny drove me around in a rented car. We passed a sign warning, 'Criminals Must Register' and Lenny started thinking out loud:

'Criminals must register. Does that mean in the middle of the hold-up you have to go to the County Courthouse and register? Or does it mean that you once committed a criminal act? Somebody goes to jail and after 15 years' incarceration, you make sure you get them back in as soon as you can by shaming anyone who would forgive them, accept them, give them employment, by shaming them on television – "The unions knowingly hired ex-convicts".'

And so Lenny decided to dedicate his book 'To all the followers of Christ and his teachings – in particular, to a true Christian, Jimmy Hoffa, because he hired ex-convicts as, I assume, Christ would have.'

Lenny was taking the drug Delaudid for lethargy, and had sent a telegram to a New York City contact referring to 'DE LAWD IN DE SKY' as a code to send a doctor's prescription. Now, in Atlantic City, he got sick while waiting for that prescription to be filled. Later, while we were relaxing on the beach, I hesitatingly brought up the subject.

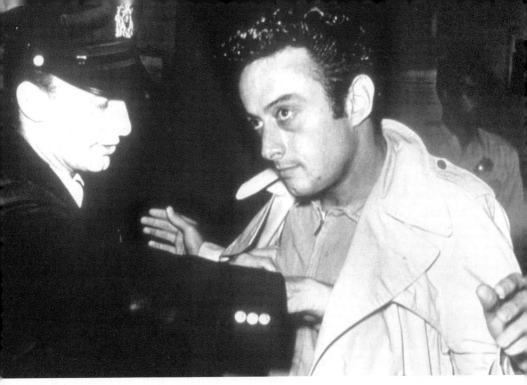

From the documentary **Lenny Bruce: Swear to Tell the Truth.**
Credit: Robert Weide, Whyaduck Productions, Inc.

'Don't you think it's ironic that your whole style should be so free-form, and yet you can also be a slave to dope?'

'What does that mean, a slave to dope?'

'Well, if you need a fix, you've got to stop whatever you're doing, go somewhere and wrap a lamp cord around your arm ...'

'Then other people are slaves to food. "Oh, I'm so famished, stop the car, I must have lunch immediately or I'll pass out."'

'You said yourself you're probably going to die before you reach 40.'

'Yeah,' he said, 'but, I can't explain, it's like kissing God.'

'Well, I ain't gonna argue with that.'

Later, though, he began to get paranoid about my role. 'You're gonna go to literary cocktail parties and say, "Yeah, that's right, I found Lenny slobbering in an alley, he would've been nothin' without me."'

Of course, I denied any such intention, but he demanded that I take a lie-detector test, and I was paranoid enough to take him literally. I told him that I couldn't work with him if he didn't trust me. We got into an argument, and I left for New York. I sent a letter of resignation to *Playboy* and a copy to Lenny. A few weeks later, I got a telegram from him that sounded as if we had been on the verge of divorce – 'WHY CAN'T IT BE THE WAY IT USED TO BE?' – and I agreed to try again.

In December 1962, I flew to Chicago to resume working with Lenny on his book. He was performing at the Gate of Horn. When I walked into the club, he was asking the whole audience to take a lie-detector test. He recognised my laugh.

Lenny had been reading a study of anti-Semitism by Jean-Paul Sartre, and he was intrigued by an item in *The Realist*, a statement by Adolf Eichmann that he would have been 'not only a scoundrel, but a despicable pig' if he hadn't carried out Hitler's orders. Lenny wrote a piece for *The Realist*, 'Letter From a Soldier's Wife' – namely, Mrs Eichmann – pleading for compassion to spare her husband's life.

Now, on stage, he peformed the most audacious piece I've ever seen by a comedian. Lenny was empathising with an orchestrator of genocide. Reading Thomas Merton's poem about the Holocaust, Lenny requested that all the lights be turned off except one dim blue spot. He then began to speak with a German accent:

'My name is Adolf Eichmann. And the Jews came every day to what they thought would be fun in the showers. People say I should have been hung. Nein. Do you recognise the whore in the middle of you – that you would have done the same if you were there yourselves? My defence: I was a soldier. I saw the end of a conscientious day's effort. I watched through the portholes. I saw every Jew burned and turned into soap.

'Do you people think yourself better because you burned your enemies at long distance with missiles without ever seeing what you had done to them? Hiroshima auf Wiedersehen. [German accent ends.] If we would have lost the war, they would have strung [President Harry] Truman up by the balls, Jim. Are you kidding with that? Not what kid told kid told kid. They would just schlep out all those Japanese mutants. "Here they did; there they are." And Truman said they'd do it again. That's what they should have the same day as "Remember Pearl Harbor". Play them in unison.'

Lenny was arrested for obscenity that night. One of the items in the Chicago police report complained, 'Then, talking about the war he stated, "If we would have lost the war, they would have strung Truman up by the balls."'

The cops broke open Lenny's candy bars, looking for drugs.

'I guess what happens,' Lenny explained, 'if you get arrested in Town A and then in Town B – with a lot of publicity – then when you get to Town C they have to arrest you or what kind of shithouse town are they running?'

Chicago was Town C. Lenny had been released on bail and was working again, but the head of the vice squad warned the manager, 'If this man ever uses a four-letter word in this club again, I'm going to pinch you and everyone in here. If he ever speaks against religion, I'm going to pinch you and everyone in here. Do you understand? You've had good people here, but he mocks the Pope – and I'm speaking as a Catholic – I'm here to tell you your licence is in danger. We're going to have someone here watching every show.'

And, indeed, the Gate of Horn's liquor licence was suspended. There were no previous allegations against the club, and the current charge involved neither violence nor drunken behaviour. The only charge pressed by the city prosecutor was Lenny Bruce's allegedly obscene performance; and his trial had not yet been held.

Chicago had the largest membership in the Roman Catholic Church of any archdiocese in the country. Lenny's jury consisted entirely of Catholics. The judge was Catholic. The prosecutor and his assistant were Catholic. On Ash Wednesday, the judge removed the spot of ash from his forehead and told the bailiff to instruct the others to do likewise. The sight of a judge, two prosecutors and 12 jurors, every one with a spot of ash on their foreheads, would have had all the surreal flavour of a Bruce fantasy.

The jury found Lenny guilty. The judge gave him the maximum penalty – a year in jail and a US$1,000 fine – 'for telling dirty jokes', in the words of one network news anchor. A week later, the case against the Gate of Horn was dismissed, but it had become obvious that Lenny was now considered too hot to be booked in Chicago again, a fear that would spread to other cities.

'There seems to be a pattern,' Lenny said, 'that I'm a mad dog and they have to get me no matter what: the end justifies the means.'

In less than two years, he was arrested 15 times. In fact, it became a news item in *Variety* when Lenny didn't get arrested one night. While the Chicago verdict was on appeal, he was working at the Off-Broadway in San Francisco. The club's newspaper ads made this offer: 'No cover charge for patrolmen in uniform.' Since Lenny had always talked on stage about his environment, and since police cars and courtrooms had become his environment, the content of his performances began to revolve more and more around the inequities of the legal system.

'In the Halls of Justice,' he declared, 'the only justice is in the halls.'

★ ★ ★

It was fascinating to watch Lenny work. 'I found this today,' he would say, introducing his audience to a bizarre concept. Then, in each succeeding performance, he would sculpt and resculpt his findings into a mini-movie, playing all the parts, experimenting from show to show like a verbal jazz musician, with a throwaway line evolving from night to night into a set routine. All Lenny really wanted to do was talk on stage with the same freedom that he exercised in his living room.

Sometimes it was sharing an insight, other times it could be just plain silliness: 'Eleanor Roosevelt had the prettiest tits I had ever seen or dreamed that I had seen. [In her voice] I've got the nicest tits that have ever been in this White House, but because of protocol we're not allowed to wear bathing suits ...'

That harmless bit of incongruity would show up in Lenny's act from time to time. One night he was arrested at the Café Au Go Go in Greenwich Village for giving an indecent performance, and at the top of the police complaint was 'Eleanor Roosevelt and her display of tits'. Lenny ended up firing all his lawyers and defending himself at his New York obscenity trial. He was found guilty – in a sophisticated city like New York. Lenny was heartbroken.

At his sentencing, the district attorney recommended that no mercy be granted because Lenny had shown a 'lack of remorse'.

'I'm not here for remorse, but for justice,' Lenny responded. 'The issue is not obscenity, but that I spit in the face of authority.'

The face of authority spat back at him that afternoon by sentencing him to four months in the workhouse.

'Ignoring the mandate of Franklin D Roosevelt,' Lenny observed, 'is a great deal more offensive than saying Eleanor has lovely nay-nays.'

On 2 October 1965, Lenny visited the San Francisco FBI head-quarters. Two days later, they sent a memo to the FBI director in Washington, describing Lenny as 'the nightclub and stage performer widely known for his obscenity'. The memo stated:

'Bruce, who advised that he is scheduled to begin confinement, 10/13/65, in New York State as a result of a conviction for a lewd show, alleged that there is a conspiracy between the courts of the states of New York and California to violate his rights. Allegedly this violation of his rights takes place by these lower courts failing to abide by decisions of the US Supreme Court with regard to obscenity.'

On 13 October (Lenny's 40th birthday), instead of surrendering to the authorities in New York, he filed suit at the US district court in San Francisco to keep him out of prison, and got himself officially declared a pauper. Since his first arrest for obscenity, his earnings had plummeted from US$108,000 to US$11,000; and he was US$15,000 in debt.

On 31 May 1966, he wrote to me, 'I'm still working on the bust of the government of New York State.' And he sent his doodle of Jesus Christ nailed to the cross with a speech balloon asking, 'Where the hell is the ACLU?'

On 3 August, while his New York obscenity conviction was still on appeal, he received a foreclosure notice on his home. Lenny died that day from an overdose of morphine, on the cusp between suicide and accident. Eighteen months later, the New York Court of Appeals upheld a lower court's reversal of his guilty verdict.

Fortunately for the record, there is a documentary, *Lenny Bruce: Swear to Tell the Truth*, which was a dozen years in the making. It was nominated for an Academy Award in 1999. But, as producer Robert Weide told me, prophetically, 'If there's a documentary about the Holocaust, it will win.' Then he added, 'The odds against my film winning are six million to one.'

Lenny really would've appreciated that. ❏

Paul Krassner is an author and political satirist. His latest book is Sex, Drugs and the Twinkie Murders: 40 Years of Countercultural Journalism *(Loompanics Unlimited); his new CD is* Campaign in the Ass *(Artemis Records)*

EDGAR LANGEVELDT

Side road, dark corner

It's easy to paint yourself into an artistic corner, harder to evade *their* clutches

Zimbabwe has had hundreds of thespians and comedy acts, but I made a bit of history for myself as the first ever stand-up comic. How? By going where previous performers feared to tread: biting, unapologetic wit and bold political satire. The sheer ferocity of it all made my routines the difference between a local church panto and Billy Connolly at full throttle.

Why? Because I was totally pissed off with my whole life and in bleak despair about the future of my country. So, like the blasphemer already roasting at the stake, I cussed and accused and railed against everything sacred and untouchable in our conservative little nation of 13 million.

It's good work if you can get it. Comedians are fêted like princes everywhere we travel, meet interesting people and get a pile of money for doing nothing more than talking a pile of shit. Much like heads of state, in fact.

Rapt audiences welcomed my exposure of South Africa's colonial legacy of race, ethnic and political tensions. And, God knows, I needed the release, too: the therapy found in a microphone and 500 watts of speakers blowing away hypocrites and poseurs, bureaucrats and bigots. Drawing from my mixed-race background, I sharpened painful points from history into assegais that drove at the heart of our eternal contradictions. I lampooned political figures until their sons and nieces pulled me aside for quiet words about how hurt they were by my eclectic social commentary. Couldn't I be more understanding of Daddy's dubious business practices or Uncle's sodomy rap?

Others wondered out loud whether I might 'disappear' like a girlfriend of a former Central Intelligence Organisation (CIO) head. Black, white, brown; they all bent low and whispered the same thing: 'Aren't you afraid that *they* will ...?'

But *they* never did. Not a whisper, not a threat. OK, a local journalist suspected of being junior level CIO did drunkenly shout me down for a joke about a Native American (he had entered the club at the end of the show and thought I was making fun of a local chief!). A well-known mouther, the crowd realised the latecomer didn't know what the hell he was talking about and hissed at him to shut up.

'You think you'll get any joy from these whites?' he snarled.

'No,' I rejoined, 'nor from you, my brother!'

After all, in African culture, the jester is free to criticise the paramount chief, where others would be executed on the spot. Under the cover of feigned insanity, the joker is the ace in society's pack, exposing, informing, advising. Even wily old Polonius sensed that there was method in Hamlet's madness.

Perhaps that is what held *them* back. So I kept pushing the limit, waiting for the terrible split second when you must choose between sitting on a hot stove or jumping from the fourth floor because you mocked a minister's inane statements about fuel prices not going up, a day before they sky-rocketed; anticipating that dread moment you're dragged away in the still of night and beaten to a pulp because you made fun of the Congo war. But that moment never came.

I was surprised at first, then relieved, then arrogant. I became a cocky trick pilot, proud holder of a valid poetic licence.

I remember looking at the tidal wave of popularity I was riding a year ago and thinking, 'Just see where this takes you. It's bigger than you. Let it do what it wants. Don't fuck with it. Grab the money, soak up the kudos, pump the hands. After years of being a starving artist, this is sweet vindication! Zimbabwe's first ever stand-up! See them queuing, breaking box-office records, signing cheques worth thousands to have *me* at their corporate dinner, fiftieth birthday, beauty pageant, product launch or golf tournament. Ha! Who said dropping out of a law degree was a foolish move? Look at me now, Ma! I'm on top of the world!'

★★★

It's 17 November 1999, 1.30am. Outside a predominantly white club. White music, white DJ, white manager, black bouncers. My black friend and I are told the place is full while dozens of white 'members' go in and out freely. This has happened here twice before. Enough is enough. 'Racism,' I scream. White manager orders black bouncers to seize me and call the police for 'disturbing the peace'. 'Great,' I laugh. 'Call ZTV and the papers too! The whole world must know what's going on here.'

Twenty minutes later, and no cops. Instead, a coloured (mixed-race) debt collector. By his own admission (as he and his well-built 'friends' bundle me into their car and promise to 'take me home') they are often hired by the club's Irish manager to 'sort out problems like me'.

Side road, dark corner:

'You're never to go back and cause shit there again.'

'I will go back. It's a racist dump.'

He hits me once. Hard. Fast. I feel blood and pieces of jawbone in my mouth. 'Why are you hitting me? Why?'

The beer in my belly and the fear in my head make my stomach empty into my pants. It's happening, it's happening: the cold sneering voice, the twisted, hate-filled face.

'You think you're clever? I saw you on SABC making fun of the president, the coloured community, everyone. You make money at other people's expense. You have to learn. Big people have wanted you dead for a long time, and tonight we're going to bury you in this field. You've got a wife and kids, haven't you?'

He notices the blood and swelling cheek and begins to twist my face in his big, fat hands. I scream at the excruciating pain. 'That's too much, man, that's too fucking much!' I wrestle him, push him away, run off before his accomplices jump out of the car. As I sprint towards the 24-hour service station to call for help and the police, I'm thinking, 'They're doing it! Jesus, they're going to kill me! For comedy? Christ? For being a fucking joker?'

The case has dragged on, one courtroom delay after another. We haven't even come to trial yet but it has given me time to consider why I was beaten up, my jaw cracked and wired for eight weeks. Was it for being a clown – maybe the ugly woman I picked on at the last show was his auntie? Or for standing up to the virtual apartheid still rampant in this world – the club in question has had bad press about racist

allegations since the day it opened? Or was I just slapped around for being a tipsy, obnoxious prima donna? Was he a bungling government hitman? Or a common heavy trying to scare the bejesus out of me by pretending to
be secret service?

It is easy to paint yourself into an artistic corner.

Every time I perform, Zimbabwean audiences expect me to attack corruption and injustice. I'm notorious for ripping apart the much hated politicians who insist on making our country look stupid. So if I jibe about dating, bad breath or computers, they are disappointed. Forget the witty, slick observations on husbands and wives: some hecklers only want to know 'what really happened at that nightclub'. I'm trapped in a circle of expectations.

In Colombia and Zimbabwe they shoot and beat up comedians. Everywhere else in the world, the stand-up comic is recognised as the acceptable face of lunacy, the suburban *pater familias* who's lost it, but in a cute and likeable way. Cute because everybody admires the canny ease of our repartee. Likeable because of the honesty inherent in our dissection of the universal experience. Many a truth is said in jest.

But truth hurts. And that is all it is really, from homey Chris Rock to homely Bill Cosby. Pain. Anger. Frustration. Despair. It drives you, it shapes you. But self-doubt also creeps in. And self-doubt leads to self-censorship. You see, I don't care any more why *they* beat me up. I just want my assailant convicted, some compensation paid for the pain and the next plane to Cape Town. I'll never live anywhere but Zimbabwe. It's my home. But I need to commute to South Africa and beyond so I can perform in more lucrative, more tolerant societies.

Needless to say, I won't be gigging in Bogotá. ❏

Edgar Langeveldt *is a stand-up comedian in Zimbabwe*

NICHOLAS LEZARD

Don't you just hate comedians?

Smug, self-satisfied and, above all, supremely rich, the contemporary comedian sits in the enchanted castle and orchestrates the group hug having sold out to the twin forces of power and money

'I like a good laugh as much as anyone.' That sentence is usually followed by the word 'but' and, funnily enough, it means the precise opposite of what it claims. As a declaration, it allows us to speculate that the person who makes it has only a rudimentary sense of humour. We know this because the person who says, 'I like a good laugh as much as anyone,' usually goes on to add that there are some kind of jokes which are beyond the pale.

What I want to say is: I like a good laugh as much as anyone, but what I no longer find funny is comedy. And this isn't because I've lost my sense of humour; its because what is delivered now under the label of comedy is simply not funny. The problem is that we laugh anyway, but only because everyone else is laughing, or because we hear around us the sound of laughter. We are living our lives over a track of canned laughs.

It is perverse to express disgruntlement with any form of creative expression in a magazine like this (I am, after all, calling for a kind of censorship), but consider the current infantile state of humour in Hollywood. Think of highly successful comedy films such as *Dumb and Dumber, There's Something about Mary* and the like. Consider the mystifying success of 'comedians' like Robin Williams and Jim Carrey, whose talents are more suitable for a seven-year-old's birthday party than for a blockbusting film supposedly watched by people old enough to vote and drive.

What these represent is not so much witless, as extremely safe comedy. All it challenges – or proposes to challenge – is a kind of one-dimensional prudery and, in this, it successfully marginalises those who dislike it as dour puritans or, at the very least, the rather boringly grown up. One is invited to assent to a relentlessly pre-adolescent obsession with genitalia and 'poo' jokes, and any dissent from the package is measured only in terms of its risk to the profitability of the medium. Which is nugatory. For if millions of teenagers will march to the multiplex to watch a woman put sperm in her hair thinking it is hair gel, why worry about those who won't?

Any notion about the sanctity of comedy itself, or its practitioners, has taken a big knock in Britain with the defection of two of its brightest stars, Ben Elton and Harry Enfield, from the BBC to privately owned Sky TV. This is more than a simple matter of parochial interest. For those who miss the nuances, the thing to remember is that these comedians began their careers more or less tied to the notion of 'alternative' comedy, the alternative being that which reacted to the bland and cosy, or worse, racially offensive comedy that prevailed at the time.

As such, these comedians were perceived as being on the left. The move from terrestrial to Murdoch-owned satellite TV is not so much an affront to the principle of not working for an unprincipled corporation, as the fact that they have sacrificed a wide and large audience for a much smaller and less heterogenous one. And the only reason one would expect them to have done that would be for the money.

What is strange is how, so far, these comedians have escaped outraged censure. For the gesture of removing yourself from four-fifths of your public in return for a pay rise is one of such contempt – and a contempt that spits in the face of what is principally understood by the concept of entertainment – that the outcry should have been louder. Maybe the outcry will be the mute one of the off-button. In Enfield's case, few people have any great expectations of his art, relying as it does on a gallery of more or less accurately observed stereotypes. Though it is ironic that the character with which he first endeared himself was a plasterer of deliciously vulgar cupidity, who was perceived as a satire on Thatcherite greed in the way he waved large bundles of cash under the noses of those poorer than himself, shouting his catchphrase: 'LOADSAMONEY'.

Those comedians who have overdrawn on our affection and respect for the way they began, by being lonely yet talented voices, may find that their funds are running low. Another erosion of our respect occurs in the field of the telethon, the mass rally of laughter which commandeers a whole day of the broadcast output, in which performers and audience are exhorted to put on clowns' red noses and, through some mysterious process, divert large sums of money from our own pockets to those of people who will administer the distribution of relief to those dying of hunger in the undeveloped world.

There are those who find my own distaste for these enterprises more offensive than I find the enterprises myself. It is an opinion I have had to brave for who, these days, would be against charity? And who can be against laughter? But, in this combined case, I am against both. First of all, dying of hunger isn't funny. It can be made to be, with a mordant or shocking or thoughtful gag, but such qualities translate poorly to the mass arena where people are being asked to dip into their pockets.

One should not risk offending anyone with a performance that might recall, say, Lenny Bruce – to think that there were once comedians whose acts were so incendiary they could be arrested (see p78). One has to play safe, to appeal to the charitable rather than the uncharitable instinct. But this goes against the very spirit of comedy, which redeems by acknowledging – and mocking – the unsatisfactory elements of our characters. To be told, instead, that we are all wonderful and generous people with a perfectly ordered set of priorities is not only nauseating and inaccurate, it may well have the opposite effect.

And now, smug, self-satisfied and supremely rich, the contemporary comedian sits in the enchanted castle and orchestrates the group hug. The castle is a large one: it's big enough for us to peer into its outlying chambers. We may even delude ourselves that we are courtiers within it. And courts need jesters. But the jests we hear now are not the troubled jokes of the licensed fool, the one who reminded rulers of their mortality, but the bland reassurances of power, the words which tell us that everything will be all right in the end, and that nothing solves problems like the marvellous, healing power of laughter. ❏

Nicholas Lezard *writes each week for the* Guardian *on books and the* Independent on Sunday *on radio. He is currently completing a book on fun for Faber & Faber due out in 2001*

Uproar!

The setting was a mission–run boarding school for girls between 12 and 18 years of age at Kashasha village, about 25 miles from Bukoba, near Lake Victoria. The first symptoms appeared on 30 January 1962 when three girls started laughing. The symptoms quickly spread to 95 of the 159 students, forcing the school to close. The school reopened, but closed again within a month after 57 pupils were stricken. Individual laugh attacks lasted from a couple of minutes to a few hours and recurred up to four times. In a few cases, the symptoms persisted for 16 days. The laugh attacks produced no fatalities or permanent after-effects, but teachers reported that students were unable to attend to their lessons for several weeks after a laughing episode.

The girls sent home from Kashasha were agents for the further spread of the laugh epidemic. Within ten days, laughter attacks were reported at Nshamba, home village for several girls. Another outbreak occurred at Ramashenye middle school on the outskirts of Bukoba, near the home of other students. The school closed when 48 of the girls were overcome with laughter. Kanyangereka village, 20 miles from Bukoba, was the site of yet another outbreak, with one of the Ramashenye girls being the source of the contagion. This flare-up first involved members of the girl's family (sister, brother, his mother-in-law and sister-in-law), but quickly spread to other villagers and to two nearby boys' schools.

Before finally abating two and a half years later, this plague of laughter spread 'like a prairie fire', forcing the temporary closure of more than 14 schools and afflicting about 1,000 people in tribes bordering Lake Victoria in Tanganyika (now Tanzania) and Uganda. Quarantine of infected villages was the only means of blocking the epidemic's advance.

The epidemic grew in a predictable pattern, first affecting adolescent females, then spreading to mothers and female relatives, but not fathers. No cases involving village headmen, policemen, schoolteachers or other 'better educated or more sophisticated people' were recorded. The laughter spread along the lines of tribal, family and peer affiliation, with females being affected the most. The greater the relatedness between the victim and the witness of the laugh attack, the more likely it was that the witness would be infected. ❏

Robert Provine is the *author of* Laughter: A Scientific Investigation *(Faber & Faber, October 2000)*

The THINKING MAN'S CHICKEN.

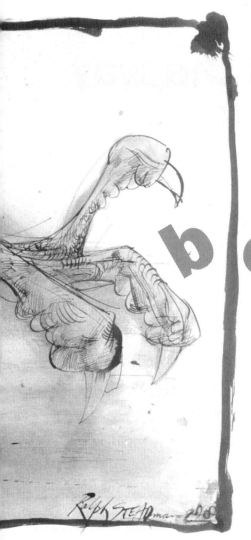

Out of bounds

*Against the assault of laughter
nothing can stand*
Mark Twain

ROGER SABIN

Larfing all the way to the dock

Censorship remains a menace to the publishers of alternative comics

The thing about the American and British underground comics of the 1960s and '70s (those deviant slices of hippie graphics) was that they weren't really 'underground'. Not in the same sense, say, as satirical comics produced in secret as a way of resisting a totalitarian state (this kind of subversion proved effective in Nazi Germany, and today continues to be severely punishable in parts of South America). They were generally available quite openly from 'headshops' and a limited number of newsstands, and went about the business of 'poking fun at the straights' without any danger of a cartoonist being shot.

Which is not to say that they didn't cause trouble, or that cartoonists and publishers didn't suffer. The brilliant satires of Robert Crumb, Gilbert Shelton, Spain Rodriguez, S Clay Wilson and others certainly hit their mark and the backlash was dramatic. It seems that 1973 was a particularly bad year. The US right-wing press had been attacking the underground on and off since its inception, but then the Supreme Court handed down a ruling whereby communities could decide their own First Amendment standards with reference to obscenity. Several busts followed, including that of *Zap*, a top anthology title famous for its Crumb content. At around the same time, a number of 'anti-paraphernalia' laws were passed, which had the effects of outlawing the sale of drug-related items and closing down the headshops. Without a sales network, the underground would have a mighty struggle to survive.

In the same year, the much lampooned corporate world took its revenge. In 1973, Disney took to court the Seattle-based *Air Pirates Funnies* – or, more specifically, *Mickey Mouse Meets the Air Pirates Funnies*

Hunt Emerson, 'AB seize it!', from Obscene issue, no. 4, 1982. Courtesy Knockabout Comics

– for depicting in its pages a pot-smoking, sexually active Mickey. Despite cartoonist Dan O'Neill's defence that a drawing has to look like its target or else the satire won't work, he and the other *Air Pirates* were accused of 'defiling Mickey's innocent delightfulness', and busted for in excess of US$1 million.

In Britain, there was a similar conservative reaction. In time, most of the hippie newspapers were prosecuted for obscenity, with the most famous case involving that man Crumb again. In 1971, *Oz* magazine was taken to the Old Bailey for its 'Schoolkids Issue', which happened to feature a sexually explicit Crumb strip, modified by the addition of the head of Rupert the Bear. This was going too far for the judge and, no doubt feeling that Rupert's 'innocent delightfulness' had been defiled, he sent the three *Oz* editors to jail (they were soon released on appeal).

One of the UK's funniest undergrounds, *Nasty Tales*, was then busted in 1973 (the *annus horribilis*). Again, the charge was obscenity; again the venue was the Old Bailey; and again Crumb was the focus (especially his 'Grand Opening of the Great Intercontinental Fuck-In and Orgy Riot'). This time the court let off the defendants with slapped wrists (they celebrated by bringing out a new issue of *Nasty Tales* which reprinted the 'Fuck-In' strip).

In spite of the pressure, the underground did survive, more or less, into the 1980s and 90s; though the counterculture changed its complexion (veering more towards direct action and green protest than the old sex, drugs and minority-causes vibe of the 1960s). New names were tried for the post-hippie comics – including 'alternative comics', 'indie comics', and 'new wave comics' – but they remained underground in spirit. The Establishment clampdowns continued. In 1982, the UK's foremost publishers of such material, Knockabout Comics, were cleared at the Old Bailey after police seized drug-related titles.

In 1996, they were again cleared in court, this time of an obscenity charge relating to – you guessed it – Robert Crumb. As star witness Paul Gravett, administrator of the Cartoon Art Trust, told the court, Crumb's work was in the tradition of Hogarth and Rowlandson and, further, he was one of the most important cartoonists of the last 25 years. That Crumb's reputation (or that of Knockabout) should have been brought into question in this way was just one more disgraceful episode to add to the list.

Simon Davies on

PRIVACY

Ursula Owen on

HATE SPEECH

Patricia Williams on

RACE

Gabriel Garcia Marquez on

JOURNALISM

John Naughton on

THE INTERNET

... all in  **INDEX**

SUBSCRIBE & SAVE

UK and overseas

○ **Yes! I want to subscribe to *Index*.**

❏ 1 year (6 issues)   £39   Save 28%

❏ 2 years (12 issues)   £74   Save 31%

❏ 3 years (18 issues)   £102   **You save 37%**

Name

Address

B0B5

£ _____ enclosed. ❏ Cheque (£) ❏ Visa/MC ❏ Am Ex   ❏ Bill me
(Outside of the UK, add £6 a year for foreign postage)

Card No.

Expiry   Signature

❏ I do not wish to receive mail from other companies.

   ✉ Freepost: INDEX, 33 Islington High Street, London N1 9BR
☎ (44) 171 278 2313   Fax: (44) 171 278 1878
e tony@indexoncensorship.org

SUBSCRIBE & SAVE

North America

○ **Yes! I want to subscribe to *Index*.**

❏ 1 year (6 issues) $52   Save 21%

❏ 2 years (12 issues) $96   Save 27%

❏ 3 years (18 issues) $135   **You save 32%**

Name

Address

B0B5

$ _____ enclosed. ❏ Cheque ($) ❏ Visa/MC ❏ Am Ex   ❏ Bill me

Card No.

Expiry   Signature

❏ I do not wish to receive mail from other companies.

   ✉ Freepost: INDEX, 708 Third Avenue, 8th Floor, New York, NY 10017
☎ (44) 171 278 2313   Fax: (44) 171 278 1878
e tony@indexoncensorship.org

Alas, the busts didn't end there. Savoy Comics, publishers based in Manchester, fared less well. Through the late 1980s and 90s, their darkly satirical comics *Meng and Ecker* and *Lord Horror* were the subject of repeated police raids (*Index* 1/1996). Prosecutions under the Obscene Publications Act followed. One hostile witness took particular exception to the former comic's use of Garfield in a story (the character Meng ejaculates over the smug feline): 'Garfield is perceived as a wholesome and endearing character,' he told the court, 'with whom all the family can identify.' The echoes of the *Air Pirates* case and the *Oz* trial were clear. In 1992, the ruling against *Meng and Ecker* was upheld, despite the efforts of defence lawyer Geoffrey Robertson QC (who had defended *Oz* in 1971), and it became the first comic to be banned in the UK. Meanwhile, the title *Lord Horror* had been published both as a book and a comic; these were prosecuted at the same time. However, whereas the book was cleared, the comic was ordered to be destroyed because, in the words of the judge, 'it might appeal to persons of a lesser intellect'.

Savoy's satire was aimed both at the right-wing Establishment and the left-wing 'politically correct brigade', and references to the Nazi Holocaust and extreme sex peppered their output during this period. Pushing the limits of anti-PC protest was a sport that other comics engaged in, too. From Atlanta, Georgia, came *Baby Sue*, a title written in the language of a redneck and containing strips that were/are blatantly racist. 'The Two Black Ladies' are characters drawn with thick lips and bunches in their hair, and who talk in pidgin English about subjects that reveal their ignorance. It would be easy to mistake the comic for a KKK publication, were it not for the fact that it comes from the same stable as a record label famous for its provocative (left-wing) punk acts. But despite this provenance, *Baby Sue* has been vilified by some fans of comics and many dealers refuse to stock it.

Racism is certainly the topic that pushes the buttons of the liberal left, and we need look no further for the King of the Wind-Up than our old friend Robert Crumb. In 1993, in an issue of the anthology title *Weirdo*, Crumb produced two strips that were to cause a major outcry. One was 'When the Niggers Take Over America!'; the other 'When the Goddamn Jews Take Over America!'. Both were gleeful stabs at the PC lobby (example from the first strip: 'Are you afraid of young black men? You oughta be ... They hate your white guts!') and traded in every racial stereotype imaginable. Inevitably, they were taken the wrong way and

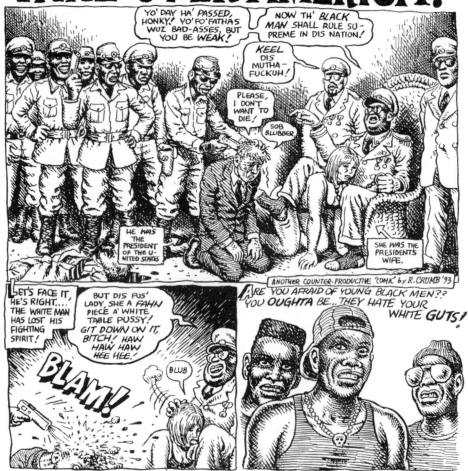

several high-profile cartoonists joined in the castigation of Crumb. For fans who had followed his career closely, however, it merely confirmed that he still had the same devilish streak that had led to all the fuss in the 1960s, 70s and 80s, and that he could still give newcomers like those over at *Baby Sue* a few lessons in outrage.

The most recent example of comics censorship has involved a title not about racism, but about children. Although *Boiled Angel* was certainly a 'humour' comic in the underground tradition, it was also strong stuff (in the S Clay Wilson manner), and included scenes of mutilation and brutal sex involving minors. Such transgressive material was in the Savoy mould, and just as likely to cause a reaction. But mild-mannered creator Mike Diana had little idea of what was in store for him when the comic was busted for obscenity in Florida. In 1995, he became the first cartoonist ever to be jailed on this charge.

Would *Boiled Angel* have caused a stink if it were in book form? Probably not: the example of *Lord Horror* indicates the double standards that apply: comics are not accorded the same leeway in terms of artistic expression as other art forms. For many of the prosecuting lawyers in the various cases outlined above, the comic is a medium that should be confined to a juvenile readership, and has no business dealing in adult satire (they'd argue that comics should indeed be comical, but in a *Beano*-like way). And if it's a source of gratification to some cartoonists and publishers that graphic humour can be such an effective 'weapon', to the point where it is clamped down on in such a systematic fashion, then censorship remains a continuing menace. In alternative comics, as ever, making people laugh can be a dangerous business. ❏

Roger Sabin is the author of two histories of comics, and co-editor of Below Critical Radar: Fanzines and Alternative Comics 1976 to 'Now' *(Slab o' Concrete Press, 2000). To find out more about censorship of comic books, see www.rpi.edu/~bulloj/search/CENSORSHIP.html*

ALAN TRAVIS

Postcard wars

With the war over and Churchill once more in power in Britain, the summer of 1953 saw a new campaign mounted against the English coast

Perhaps the title of most unlikely target ever of the British censors was Donald McGill, king of the saucy postcard. Yet during an anti-vice crusade waged by Churchill's post-war Tory government, the ordinary British family was not even allowed to enjoy his cheeky seaside humour when they went on holiday.

In the summer of 1953, sweetshops and newsagents in Bournemouth, Cleethorpes, Folkestone, Llandudno, Margate, Poole, Ramsgate, Swanage, Weymouth and Ryde on the Isle of Wight all found themselves branded as criminals by the smut-hounds for selling postcards containing the kinds of awful puns and double entendres that have been swapped in school playgrounds for decades.

Each town had its own 'censorship committee' and only Blackpool and the Isle of Man were prepared to tolerate smutty jokes about young lovers and fat ladies. This was a serious crackdown. In September 1953, the Lincolnshire police, acting under the orders of the Director of Public Prosecutions, raided 16 stationers' shops in Cleethorpes alone. Some 5,405 postcards, which had been on sale all summer, were seized from their racks along with 15 rubber dolls, or 'novelties' as the official records described them.

More than 165 different cards were condemned, including 30 by McGill himself, and six card companies were charged with unlawfully publishing obscene postcards. McGill, a man already in his 70s, found himself in the dock at Lincoln Quarter Sessions on a charge under the 1857 Obscene Publications Act. At that time there was no defence based on artistic or literary merit on the statute book. That came later, in the amended act of 1959.

"Gentlemen's Requisites? Yes, Sir, go right through 'Ladies' Underwear'!"

"I suppose you're giving him all he wants?"
"Oh, Doctor, he's been far too ill to think about anything of that sort!"

McGill told the court he had his first card published when he was 16 and his defence counsel argued the cards were not obscene but were 'traditional English music-hall vulgarity which has stood the test of many years'.

But the court was not impressed. McGill was heavily fined and the offending cards sent off to the furnace. One that was declared obscene and attracted a £5 fine involved a man walking into a newspaper office:

'I want you to put this notice of the birth of my son in your paper.'

'Yes, sir. How many insertions?'

'Mind your own business.' ❑

Alan Travis is home affairs editor of the Guardian *and author of* Bound and Gagged: the secret history of obscenity in Britain *(www.profile books.co.uk, August 2000)*

"She's a nice girl. Doesn't drink or smoke, and only swears when it slips out!"

"I've some good news for you, Mrs. Lovejoy!"
"Miss Lovejoy, Doctor."
"Oh, well, I've some bad news for you, Miss Lovejoy!!"

Credit for all four McGill postcards reproduced here: Pharos International Ltd

SAEED OKASHA

Opiate of the masses

Has the state's control of comedy taken away Egypt's once legendary sense of humour?

When comedy film star Ala Walieddin decided to change the title of his latest film *Al Nazer Salaheddin* – a punning reference to the Kurdish Muslim general Saladin who liberated Jerusalem from the hands of the Crusaders – to merely *Al Nazer,* he explained himself publicly.

According to an interview in *Sabah Al Kheir*, the reason goes back to a journalist who claimed that Walieddin, his producer and director, conspired with Israeli Prime Minister Ehud Barak to defame the 'Arab' hero. Complaining that parodying Salaheddin only serves Israel's goal, the journalist said the title was deliberately chosen at a time when Israel seeks to plant 'the seeds of despair in Arab souls' to dissuade them from even thinking about regaining Jerusalem. Other critics had voiced similar concerns. Fearing repercussions – financial or otherwise – Walieddin shortened the name of the film before Egypt's censorship authority had the chance to do it for him.

The politicisation of comedy is not new. For the last 50 years, whether it is criticising state policy or used by the authorities to endorse it, comedy has been the most influential and popular artistic form.

It all began in 1953, with the film *Antar and Liblib*, starring Shokoko, Serag Mounir and Ahlam. The plot took the traditional story of the competition between a strong, rich tyrannical personality, in this case Antar, and the poor, weak Liblib, over the heart of the beautiful girl next door. Beneath the facile plot, the film made great use of double entendres to treat one of the major political issues of the day: the departure of British troops from Egypt and the reclaiming of Egypt's lands. One memorable scene has Liblib confronting Antar over their common love interest and demanding 'the funds and canal' owed to him. When a perplexed Antar asks him what he means, Liblib responds that he means the bride price and the 'canal of love'. As romantic comedy and political allegory, the film was extremely successful, and it was not lost on the audience that Liblib's ultimate victory over Antar stood for more than just matters of the heart.

It was, perhaps, as a result of the success of *Antar and Liblib* that President Gamal Abdel Nasser discovered the importance of comedy in promoting state policy. Soon after instituting military conscription, he charged funny man Ismail Yassin with making a series of films to encourage Egyptian youth to join the armed forces. There followed a series of slapstick comedies starring Private Ismail, starting with the 1957 production *Ismail Yassin in the Army*, then *Ismail Yassin in the Air Force* and *Ismail Yassin in the Navy*. With their portrayal of the lighter side of draft life, Yassin's films were a great help in persuading young men to join the army rather than avoid military service.

The state's use of comedy to instil certain values or ideas in the public consciousness continued throughout Nasser's reign. Between 1960 and 1967, the state-run General Cinema Authority produced a number of films starring Shuyikar and Fouad Al Mohandis, including *Airport of Love*, *The Ambassador's Wife* and *His Highness*. All exemplified the ingenuity and bravado of Egyptian politicians and police in dealing with the superpowers – or in exposing conspiracies that threatened the country's security.

Following the 1967 war with Israel, a number of light comedies, heavily dependent on farce, appeared at Nasser's instigation to help bring Egyptian society out of its post-defeat depression.

Cheering Egyptians up wasn't the only motive behind making these films, however. It was also an attempt to stop the wave of political jokes that followed defeat. About a month after the war, Nasser asked Egyptians to stop making fun of their leaders. Giving them something else to laugh at was more effective than exhortations. Some of the films even co-opted and neutralised the same popular jokes, making them part of the acceptable political and artistic landscape, and putting a lid on the jokers.

Following Nasser's death in 1970 and the victorious 1973 war, Egyptian cinema was overwhelmed with films criticising the dead

Abdel Imam rising above a sea of censorship

leader's regime. As for comedy, farce – entirely free of political and
social content – ruled the day. The reason for this was the state's
withdrawal from the Cinema Authority in 1973: while it no longer had
any interest in producing ideologically sound comedies, it kept an ever
more watchful eye on films from the private sector which was loath to
take on the state with politically charged films, comedies or otherwise.
Those who did suffered the consequences. Youssef Chahine's 1972
production, *The Sparrow*, lasted two days before it was pulled.

It was around this time that the star of Abdel Imam rose in the
firmament. He appeared in a string of film farces such as *Sha'aban
Below Zero* and *The Search for Scandal*. But it was in the theatre, less
subject to censorship than film, that he made his mark. The 1973
production *School of Troublemakers*, starring Imam, contained a bitter
critique of Egypt's lost generation. In 1976, Imam took an even more
daring step by starring in the comedy *A Witness Who Saw Nothing*, in
which he spoke openly of the sad state of economic and social affairs.
The play made open fun of President Anwar Al Sadat which, in turn,

landed Imam in front of a court which sentenced him to three months in prison. Had it not been for his fame, and fear of a popular reaction, the sentence might have been carried out. *A Witness Who Saw Nothing* became one of Egypt's most successful plays ever: it ran continuously until 1986 and brought Imam unprecedented stardom.

Over the past few years, a new generation of comedians has attempted to imitate Imam but with little success. With rare exceptions, the scathing humour of the theatre of the 1970s and early 80s is totally absent from the film comedies of today. The 1998 film *Saidi* marked the return of political comedy but on a much more superficial level. It featured the burning of the Israeli flag with an approving state security officer looking on. The scene provoked waves of applause from audiences, but the message was clear: the state will allow only symbolic feel-good political content.

It is the triteness with which the subject is treated that has led some commentators – even those against normalisation of ties with Israel, for example – to criticise the exploitation of political themes in many comedies. Essam Zakariya, writing for *Sabah Al Kheir* in July,

Hand-on-mouth comedy from Nasser's Egypt

commented on the hackneyed treatment of politics and the Arab–Israeli conflict in such films as *Hamam in Amsterdam* and *Aboud at the Border*.

The issue that remains open today is how to make good comedies that deal with political issues – on whatever side of the fence – without descending into banality. Meanwhile, it is increasingly difficult to get subjects that are at odds with state policy – or, indeed, that are anything more than mindless trivia – past the censor. Comedies that threaten to broach politically sensitive or critical issues are not given the green light. A prime example was the comedy proposed last year that was to have centred on a couple of friends, one Muslim and one Copt. It was turned down by the Censorship Authority with scarcely a moment's thought.

No matter what form it takes, comedy is a political act in the first degree. It serves as an outlet for frustrations and is a way of putting impossible and incomprehensible situations into perspective. Egyptian society today is urgently in need of such therapy. Writing in *Al Wafd*, Sami Abou Al Ezz asked: 'Where have all the smiles gone? Why all the long faces? Has there been a change among Egyptian citizens so that they are no longer willing to laugh?'

Israel's former defence minister, Moshe Dayan, put it somewhat differently: 'I would not fear the Egyptians even if they possessed nuclear weapons. But I will begin to feel nervous when they stop making jokes about themselves and about others.' The underlying meaning is that the society that doesn't laugh could explode at any minute. ❏

Saeed Okasha is a staff writer for the Cairo Times, *in which a version of this article first appeared*

YAVLINSKY I know.
KIRIENKO Where are we
going?
YAVLINSKY We've just arrived.
*The vault. Enormous ancient
tomes.*
YAVLINSKY (*blowing off the dust*)
Ah! Here is what will save us.
We need to know who he is
and then we shall be able to
vanquish his magic.

5. *A large hall.*
*Putin in the uniform of a privy
councillor (covered in stars and
ribbons) is giving a speech to a
lot of bureaucrats.*
PUTIN I am warning you
of the danger of subversive
activity! Now as never before
we must heighten our
vigilance!
Applause.
SHAIMIEV The way he said
that! The devil!
PUTIN And underpin our
productivity!
ZHIRINOVSKY He's a Spinoza,
no two ways about it, a Spinoza.
SELEZNEV Anti-Dühring!
ZYUGANOV Ulyanov-Lenin!

*Behind the scenes at NTV: Yeltsin, Lushkov
(mayor of Moscow and one-time presidential hopeful)
and another in* Kukly *guise take a break*

PUTIN Moreover, not one instance of indifference, red tape, or
indiscipline on the part of government officials must be allowed to pass
unpunished ...
Ovation, shouts of 'Bravo!'
LUZHKOV (*to Primakov*) The man's given us all new heart!
PRIMAKOV (*swallows a pill*) I think I may need one.

6. *Early morning. Putin gets up and tiptoes stealthily out to the garden. He is being watched from behind a fence by Yavlinsky and Kirienko, who suddenly removes binoculars from his eyes.*

KIRIENKO I don't believe it!

YAVLINSKY What?

KIRIENKO There's some sort of UFO!

Through the binoculars Putin is seen and, hovering above him like a dragonfly, Berezonvsky.

BEREZOVSKY Hello, young fellow! I'll just comb your hair once more with the magic television comb. I'll soon have you looking good enough to eat.

All this is being observed by Yavlinsky and Kirienko from behind the bushes.

YAVLINSKY I understand everything now! Do you see those three red hairs on his head?

KIRIENKO Yes.

YAVLINSKY We have to pull them out!

KIRIENKO Oh, no, don't do that He'll be completely bald and really frightening.

YAVLINSKY But he will also lose his magic power over our city!

7. *Putin at the theatre, on stage in short polka-dot trousers, singing in a lewd manner.*

PUTIN 'My old man says follow the van, and don't dilly-dally on the way ...'

In the semi-darkness the auditorium is packed.

SHAIMIEV How he can sing! The devil!

PUTIN (as seen through the eyes of the audience) is on stage dressed all in white and singing in a faultless voice, in Italian, 'O sole mio'.

In the wings − Yavlinsky and Kirienko.

KIRIENKO Who's going to pull his magic hairs out?

YAVLINSKY (*getting his tweezers out*) I am.

KIRIENKO Good man! (*Shakes his hand.*) Farewell!

8. *On stage, Putin in polka-dot pants.*

PUTIN 'Off went the van with me 'ome packed in it, I followed on with me old cock linnet ...'

Yavlinsky emerges with tweezers emerges from the wings and quickly plucks the three hairs from Putin's head.

Shouting, tumult among the audience. On stage instead of a handsome man wearing a white tuxedo stands a malign little Putin in polka-dot short pants. Shouts from the audience.

'How ghastly!'

'What the hell is going on?'

'This is not Zinnober!'

'It's that horrible little Zaches!'

'Get him off the stage!'

Tomatoes are thrown at the stage.

BEREZOVSKY (*in a box*) Oh, dear, oh, dear! What a mess! We really must adjust his image straight away.

He flies out in his fairy form, but Yavlinsky takes aim and fires at him with a catapult. Berezovsky falls with a shriek into the orchestra pit.

ALL Bravo! Bravo, our hero!

A beaming Yavlinsky bows, making a smooth gesture with his hand and …

9. *… the same gesture causes the book by Hoffmann to fall from his hand. Yavlinsky opens his eyes. He is lying in bed, the lamp still lit above him. It is morning. Yavlinsky sits up in bed and yawns.*

YAVLINSKY The things you dream …

Pours a glass of tea. Turns on the radio.

NEWSREADER'S VOICE Today under the wise leadership of the acting President of the Russian Federation, Vladimir Vladimirovich Putin, a meeting has been convened of top officials of the ministry of internal affairs and external debt. Top of the agenda will be measures for the immediate bringing forward of spring in the interests of the Russian people. The anti-terrorist operation in Chechnya is continuing successfully … Losses by the federal forces are minimal …

The voice of the newsreader is gradually overlaid by another voice singing the last bars of 'O sole mio!' in Italian. ❏

With thanks to NTV. Kukly can be seen on NTV's international service, broadcast on Hot Bird 2 *(digital TV). Telephone number for enquiries in the UK is 0800 028 1175. Translated by Arch Tait*

MARK NESBIT

Dead funny

Cartoons can seriously damage your health

On Wednesday, 22 July 1987, in St Ives Street, Chelsea, London, **Naji el-Ali** was shot at close range by a lone gunman while going to work at *Al-Qabas* newspaper. Five weeks later, still in a coma, the most influential Middle Eastern cartoonist died aged 51.

Naji el-Ali was a Palestinian. Born in 1936 in Galilee, he moved with his family to Ein-Al-Helwe refugee camp in southern Lebanon following the establishment of Israel in 1948. He spent the rest of his life in exile, most of it shuttling between Beirut and Kuwait. In 1985 he was expelled from Kuwait and spent his last two years in London.

His stark, symbolic cartoons portrayed the bitter struggle of the Palestinians against Israeli occupation. He also campaigned against the absence of democracy, widespread corruption and gross inequality in the Arab world. His cartoons remain as relevant today as they were then.

El-Ali's 'signature' was the barefoot boy, Hanzala (right), whom he regarded as his conscience. He received numerous death threats during his life but the prophetic cartoon *Achilles Heel* was drawn after a telephoned warning a few days before he was finally shot.

Both before and since Naji el-Ali's death many more cartoonists around the world have been murdered because of their work. On 2 July 1993, **Asaf Koçak** (left), a 34-year-old cartoonist, was burned to death in the city of Sivas in Turkey when thousands of Muslim fundamentalists staged a protest against 'progressive' artists participating in a festival. They set fire to a hotel. Koçak, a humanist who used his cartoons to fight

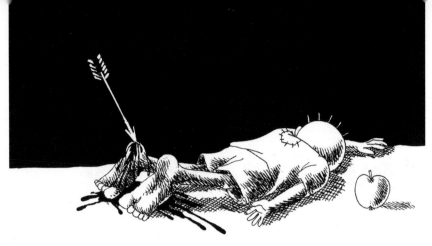

Naji el-Ali, Achilles Heel

illiteracy, exploitation, fundamentalism, torture and injustice, was one of 36 people killed.

On Saturday, 2 September 1995, **Guerrovi Brahim**, a cartoonist for the pro-government Algerian daily *El Moudjahid* was kidnapped and found executed near his home in a southern suburb of Algiers.

Severe but lesser sanctions against cartoonists and those who publish them have included floggings and long terms of imprisonment. In 1992, **Manouchehr Karimzadeh** was sentenced by Iran's revolutionary court to 50 lashes, one year in prison and a fine of 500,000 rials for a cartoon the authorities claimed bore an unacceptably close resemblance to Ayatollah Khomeini, and appeared to have a hand missing – a reference to Islamic-style punishment. After he'd served the sentence, the Supreme Court ruled that he was to be retried and a further arbitrary ten-year sentence was imposed; Karimzadeh was quietly released after two years.

On Sunday 7 March 1993, an episode of *BC* (overleaf) drawn by Johnny Hart and syndicated through the American Creators Syndicate resulted in the imprisonment of the editor and editor-in-chief of *Arab News* in Jeddah, Saudi Arabia. **Balaram Menon**, the editor was sentenced to two years in prison and 500 lashes, while his editor-in-chief, **Farouk Luqman**, received a one-year sentence and 300 lashes. The Saudi authorities felt the episode questioned the

Manouchehr Karimzadeh

Johnny Hart, BC

existence of God. Following considerable international publicity the two were granted a royal pardon on 14 September.

In our media-saturated world, it's easy to lose sight of the immense power of the black-and-white cartoon on the printed page, but in most other parts of the world it is still seen as a real force for change. This is, of course, well understood by those in power. Which is why, in places like Burma, and even in more open societies like Egypt, Turkey or Iran, cartoonists continue to feel the full force of censorship. ❏

Mark Nesbit is an award-winning Irish cartoonist. His 1995 study on cartoon censorship formed the basis of Index's *website Cartoon Gallery. His work can be seen on http://www.autografix.com*

For more information see the newly updated Censored Cartoon Gallery on the Index *website: http://www.indexoncensorship.org. We are always pleased to include new or updated information*

SALIL TRIPATHI

The land that lost its laugh

M ANY YEARS LATER, as he switched off the television set after
watching an old Charlie Chaplin rerun on the late-night channel
at his daughter's home in Sydney, Sugumaran Ganasegaran remembered
that warm afternoon when he outlawed jokes.

That was on the island, not in this large, polyglot city by the sea
that had become his home. He was a senior government officer then,
responsible for the department of citizenship. There had been rumblings
about how widespread the problem had become, but since these were
merely rumours passed furtively around water coolers and in coffee
shops, he thought nothing of it. By the time he heard about it, what
had been a harmless recreation had become an obsession, a full-blown
disease. It was everywhere: on street corners, in public gardens, in
factories. Production supervisors frowned as they watched workers take
off protective masks in working hours and fall about laughing. Even
airline flights were delayed as pilots, with tears of laughter streaming
down their cheeks, struggled to come to grips with the controls,
rendered unhinged and incapable by the joke about the Great Leader
and the missing parachute.

It seems the Great Leader was flying with Reagan, the Pope, a hippie
and an Australian pilot. Suddenly, the pilot announced that the plane was
losing height and, as there were only four parachutes, he was taking the
first one and leaving, because he had a girlfriend waiting in Bali. The
plane lost 1,000 feet. Reagan said since he was the leader of the free
world, he must leave next to save the world from communists. And he
left with the second parachute. The plane lost another 3,000 feet; there
were now two parachutes and three people. The Great Leader looked
at the Pope and the dopey-eyed backpacker. 'I shall go next,' he said.
'Although my country is the smallest in the world, I am the smartest

man in the country; without me, the country will founder, and without my country, the world will founder.' And, so saying, he left. The Pope looked at the hippie and said that perhaps he should go next since he had his whole life ahead of him, to regret, confess and repent. He, being God's man, could meet his maker. The hippie smiled and said, 'Actually there are still two parachutes left: the Great Leader plunged to earth wearing my backpack.' And then the pilots would laugh themselves hoarse, fall all over the instrument panels and fail to get lift-off.

Economists were warning of declining productivity; companies had given advanced warnings to stock markets that their financial results in the next quarter might decline; analysts on the grand avenue fronting the bay, home to the city's financial bodies, had begun to revise their forecasts downwards; fickle foreign money was threatening to flee.

Why, that very morning, when Sugumaran Ganasegaran was speeding to work, he was stopped by a traffic policewoman, eminently desirable in her bright red lipstick, tight black trousers, shining helmet, dark glasses and bulging chest covered by that white jacket. She got off her motorbike, forming a neat arc bursting with erotic possibilities. But when she found he was a senior bureaucrat, she told him the one about the bureaucrats.

'Two bureaucrats from the ministry of national planning were walking in the forest, looking for a place to stay the night. There was nothing in sight except a lone hut with its flickering light. Boldly, they knocked on the door. Seeing strangers, the farmer was reluctant to let them in, assuming they must be illegal immigrants. When they said they were willing to do anything if he would allow them to spend the night, he showed them to the stable. It was a stinking mess. "Could you clean it up?"

'The two bureaucrats looked at each other and, "Of course, no problem." They'd cleaned up their country once, so what was a mere stable? The next morning, when the farmer went to the stable, it smelled like heaven! Not only was it spick and span, but a delicious lavender fragrance floated in the air. Embarrassed and pleased, he said they could stay another night, as many nights as they wanted, but would they come and help him set the table for breakfast? "Sure," the two said, and followed him with an air of rewards well earned. They arrived and the farmer's wife said, "Set the table." "But how do we do that?" one of them asked. And the wife replied, "You decide." The two looked at each other glumly, and then, hesitantly, one of them ventured, "We are bureaucrats from the city. Tell us what to do. We can clean up any shit you want, but don't ask us to take any decisions.'"

Saying this, she burst out laughing and, holding her stomach, mounted her motorbike and vanished with a mighty roar.

No place was safe; it was an epidemic. Jokes were sprouting around the city like bamboo shoots after monsoon rains. Sugumaran was told that chain letters were being circulated, with jokes in them, like the one about the Great Leader going fishing with the leader of the neighbouring state. At the end of the day, it seemed, the Great Leader had nothing to show, while the neighbouring leader had a neat pile of fish. 'What am I doing wrong?' the Great Leader asked. 'Nothing,' said the neighbour. 'But even the fish don't dare open their mouths when you're around.'

By the time he too had received one of the infamous letters, Sugumaran Ganasegaran was really worried. If it went on like this, chaos lay ahead. At a meeting with his colleagues yesterday, when he had asked them their opinion about the neighbouring state building a bigger and better airport, even they had started giggling. 'This is not a laughing matter, the threat is serious,' he had said. But one of his colleagues began: 'Their boss took a Somali, a Russian and an American to a nice restaurant in the city. Looking at the menu, the American said, "Gee, the cost of food here is quite high. What's your opinion?" At this, the Somali asked: "Food? What's that?" The Russian asked: "Cost? What's that?" And the boss asked: "Opinion? What's that?"'

This was sheer blasphemy! Dissent had always been snuffed out in the city. But how could you outlaw jokes? They were pernicious: they captured the subterranean mood and spread like wildfire, from friend to friend, in coffee shops, at bus stands and in emails. In fact, the city's email network was grinding to a halt because everyone was sending jokes to everyone else. The liberals had long argued that laughter was an effective safety valve, but now the valve had fallen off.

SUGUMARAN liked modern technology: it put you in control of things. But the jokes had spun everything out of control. The idea of making the Internet accessible to every man, woman and child was to enable people to communicate more effectively and make his job of surveillance easier, not to trade jokes. The mighty Internet was gridlocked. There was no escape: the moment you logged on, the jokes began, creating an enormous traffic jam.

Traffic jam! Why hadn't he thought of it before? Among the many superlative things his city was famous for – an efficient port and airport, a squeaky clean subway system, clean administration, competitive economy and the world's best record of strike-free production – was an incredibly efficient transport system. Traffic jams happened in Bangkok and Bombay, not in his city. Why couldn't he apply the same model to this problem?

Like prostitution, jokes were a part of the human condition, a necessary evil. They could not be banned outright, for they would go underground, making their control even harder. Why not ration jokes? Each person could tell one joke a day, and read one joke a day. Gatherings of more than four people at street corners would be prohibited. A joke could only be forwarded once, to no more than three people. Violations would be punishable by fines.

Email software at Internet servers would be modified so that a joke could be sent to only three people daily; if another attempt were made, the system would disable and the email crash. If people persisted, after one warning, the system would wipe out the hard disk.

For those with the urge to listen to more than one joke a day, a new system was planned. Drafted in best bureaucratic manner, his note read:

'If the government takes firm action against the sending and receiving of humorous emails it might send the wrong signal to the markets, especially at a time when the government wants to attract investors from Silicon Valley. A more appropriate policy would be to rationalise the use of jokes, based on our effective policy to control the number of cars on the streets. If the government does not act now, the consequences could be dangerous in the long run, with investment meant for the country drying up and going to our rivals. To prevent that, effective action must be taken urgently.

'There are two factors regarding the management of perceptions abroad. The liberal western press will ridicule any action against electronic transmission of jokes, but businesses would welcome such a move. There is also the negative fallout of businesses thinking we are not a serious people if they find that most people go to the Internet to send and receive jokes.

'So we should not ban jokes outright, but regulate their use. The solution lies in creating a scarcity and assigning monetary value to the perception of scarcity. The government should insist on people bidding for certificates of entitlement to tell or receive additional jokes directly through the Internet, on a secure server, which would accept major credit cards. Weekly quotas will be announced on the website of the Department of Citizenship and the market will become more transparent. It will not be rumour-driven, and people will be able to make their assessment on the movement of prices. The product, chosen randomly, will be delivered via email.

'This way, the government will raise revenue, identify those citizens who are in the habit of sending and receiving jokes and, by assigning monetary cost to telling and receiving jokes, the government will send a sound message to the citizens: the Internet is not a laughing matter, and there is no substitute for hard work. If we treat the Internet as a giant coffee house, we shall swiftly become waiters, not patrons.'

Satisfied, he sent the proposal off to the cabinet. It was accepted instantly and the new policy was in place within a week. The city became the first place in the world to regulate the supply of jokes. Productivity rose again, stock markets soared, foreign investment shot up, the Internet functioned smoothly and the trains ran on time. ❑

Salil Tripathi *is a London-based writer working on a novel set in Southeast Asia. He writes frequently for* Index.

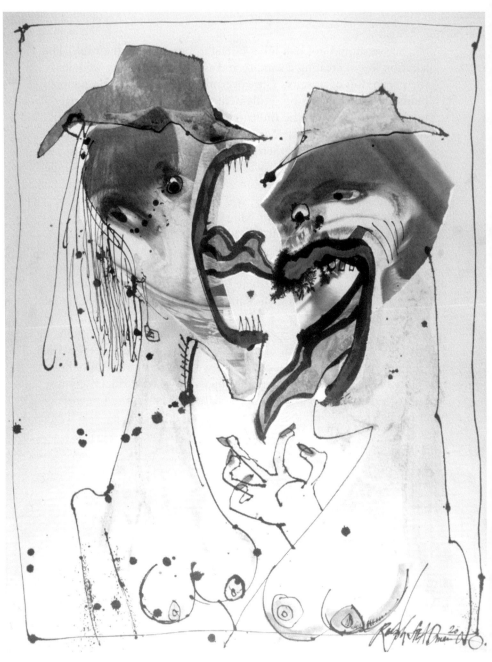

Gossip

No laughing matter

*Life does not cease to be funny when people die
any more than it ceases to be serious when people laugh*
George Bernard Shaw

ART SPIEGELMAN

Walking gingerly, remaining close to our caves

People tell Art Spiegelman he makes them laugh. He says he doesn't really understand humour and is only trying to tell his particular set of truths in the hope that there's 'some resonance beyond the laughs'. He describes his most serious work, *Maus,* which has appeared in 21 countries, as both a 'diaspora novel' and part of the 'comix' genre

By working with comix, I can ratiocinate. They get to fly below critical radar, and thereby go into your head. Comix echo the way we think, in the sense that thought takes place in bursts of language and in icons that exist in one's head. Comix are about the only medium I can think of that accurately does that. Talking strictly as an outside observer, after the initial, much more intuitive genuine impulses that moved me through all this, I would say that since comix are a way of showing time spatially, they have advantages in terms of trying to palimpsest the past and the present into the same narrative.

A lot of humour comes from taboo. Maybe all humour ultimately comes from some version of taboo, and then one has to gauge how funny is it, and how efficacious at doing something other than just making you laugh. There's a lot of laughter that comes from the nervousness of 'oh, jeez! you're not supposed to say that and you said it'.

I was watching a show called *Politically Correct* after the political debates, and one of the panellists asked, 'Why is our military budget so high? We don't have any enemies any more.' And another more conservative member of the panel says, 'What about China?' and then Gore Vidal says, 'A great laundry people.' It's funny, but in a way you wouldn't have dared do that if the enemy was Israel and you were to say, 'They're great pawnbrokers,' or an African nation and you said, 'All great singers and dancers.' The Chinese and Japanese don't have as good a lobby [as the Jews] for sensitising people to these things. The more sensitised the community, the more difficult it is to make the jokes. The joke here is about conjuring up stereotypes.

Ultimately, cartooning is a conservative business, even when you have so-called liberal and radical cartoonists. Almost by definition, cartooning tends to use stereotypes: you're dealing with a recognisable iconic picture. It ends up saying, 'Yep, those Chinese really are good at laundry, ha.' But it doesn't tell you how to get past that. Much harder to take that stereotype and do some kind of judo turn with it that actually undoes it. And when you do, then you're in dangerous territory.

I had a cover that was first accepted and then rejected with horror by the *New Yorker* at the tail-end of the OJ Simpson trial. I drew something that portrayed 'the race card', since this was exploited repeatedly throughout the trial by OJ's lawyers. It ended up in the *Nation* instead – but minus the caption. The idea of showing OJ with a minstrel face was not about reaffirming 'all blacks are watermelon-eating coons', but a way of showing that he was playing himself up as a black victim. It's a paint job, as much a mask as the Klan mask on the Los Angeles Police Department. One thing that makes it so complicated is that I'm not black, therefore I don't have the right to say certain things; though, in the same issue of the *New Yorker* that this was destined for, Maya Angelou describes the OJ trial as a minstrel show.

I certainly wouldn't subscribe to the notion that the only person with the authority to speak is the most directly affected. That would be to say, 'It's a hermetically closed subject, don't pay attention, don't listen, it's strictly among us insiders.' It can't be that way. It's a matter of how sensitive and intelligent the commentator is. *Life is Beautiful* made me bristle, not because he wasn't Jewish, but because, ultimately, it's kind of stupid. And *Schindler's List* made me bristle because Spielberg was kind of stupid – it's equal opportunity stupidity. One Jew, one not.

Everybody moves through this territory attempting to bend it, evoking the Holocaust for different reasons. That's why I tried to stay very, very blinkered while working: all I was trying to do was understand

1995, Art Spiegelman's contentious response to the OJ trial, rejected by the New Yorker, *accepted by the* Nation, *but minus the caption*

what my father was telling me and keep that the focus. I wouldn't make any other grand claims for what *Maus* was. I certainly never expected it to be 'Holocaust for beginners'; I never meant either to trivialise or aggrandise the survivor: it was just a matter of me dealing with my own family crucible, which isn't to say it's the only way one can move through this terrain, but it certainly was what was given me to do.

Because there's so much blood and pain, it seems reasonable to walk gingerly. I used metaphor to try to understand the genocide, but I didn't turn the genocide into a metaphor. The thing about *Maus* is that it's a diaspora novel, not a Zionist novel. It's about a destiny that exists in which Israel hardly figures, as opposed to most popular American culture about the Holocaust that posits Israel as some kind of happy ending, like *Schindler's List*, where the survivors get to end their story in Israel: the payback for the Holocaust is getting a homeland. To me, this is kind of a booby prize. When you've proved that nationalism is an absolutely virulent disease, the solution isn't to give the people who got clobbered a nation, it's something else.

We went through this thing in the last century that knocked the underpinnings out of our civilisation. We live as if the Enlightenment still held, and yet there's this demonstrable, gaping hole in the centre that says, 'actually we're far closer to the caves than the moon', and clearly, we're capable of getting there again. Maybe Bosnian Muslims this time instead of Jews. It was such a large-scale failure of civilisation that it can't help but stay as a traumatised arena.

I'm not a humorist. I read all these books on the psychoanalytic theory of humour to try to understand. Nevertheless, I find I make people laugh, and I don't understand why. If you keep saying something that you perceive is true, occasionally people laugh because you're saying something you're not supposed to say. I'm more interested in irony than in humour. For me it has to do with measuring the distance between what's said and what's meant. ❑

Art Spiegelman was interviewed by Natasha Schmidt

Art Spiegelman, Maus: A Survivor's Tale, *1986; from Chapter 2, 'Auschwitz (Time Flies)'*

SCOTT CAPURRO

Comfort zones

Political correctness and the dumbing down of the media are killing comedy

Whenever I'm trying to fill an hour of stand-up for the Edinburgh Festival, the last thing I wonder is, 'Jeez, will this set land me a spot on television?' The reasons are twofold: first, I do what makes me laugh, otherwise I get bored; second, I've done stand-up on television and it ain't the apex of my career. Television producers and editors seem to have an uncanny knack for siphoning the humour out of just about anything, especially the royals, and particularly the pretty, dead ones.

Yet television comedy is held in some oddly high regard as a move up for a comic. I guess that's because if you can't get a TV profile going, your live shows in the provinces don't sell very well. Why should someone in, say, Leeds, come and see you at the Varieties if you aren't good enough to be on *Les Dawson*?

But to be on *Les*, or any television programme, your set must be 'clean'. Which means few or no dirty words. Misogyny within social norms, fine, but save the word 'cunt' for the wife beatings, mate. That's right. No 'cunts', although the halls of the BBC are teeming with them. Which is sad, since 'cunt' is plainly the most versatile word in the English language. It's a verb, a noun, an adjective, and it's really the last word on earth that, no matter how it's used, makes my mother angry. One is also discouraged from using the word 'fuck' on television, particularly as a verb. Particularly if you're gay.

See, as an out cocksucker, there are lots of things I can get away with on stage but, on television, I'm already perceived as dangerous. TV companies treat me, in rehearsal for a taping, as though I'm retarded or a child or, worse yet, American. 'Please be *nice*, Mr Capurro. You want the people watching to like you, don't you? Good. We wouldn't want everyone to think that you're *naughty*, would we?'

Credit: Kent Taylor

Then they go through the litany of words I'm not supposed to use. When the show is edited and televised, other comics' 'fucks' are left in. Mine are removed. After all, being gay is dirty enough. Do I have to be dirtier with my dirty mouth?

I'm not really complaining. I've learned to manoeuvre my way throughout television. I can play the spiky-but-warm, take-the-cock-out-of-my-mouth-and-press-the-tongue-to-my-cheek game with squeamishly positive results. Usually. But in Australia, during the taping of a 'Gala' to honour a comedy festival in Melbourne, the director had a *grand-mal* seizure when I described Jesus as a 'queer-wannabe'. I saw papers fly up over the heads of a stunned, strangely silent audience. Later I found out it was the director's script. Apparently they found him after the show, huddled in a corner, crying like a recently incarcerated prisoner who'd just taken his first 'shower'.

He was afraid I'd pollute minds, I suppose. At least that's what he told his assistant. So now, TV is promoting itself as a politically correct barometer? A sort of big-eyed nanny looking out for our sensitive sensibilities? In the six years that I've been performing in the UK, I've seen political correctness catch on like an insidious disease, like a penchant for black, like the need to oppress. Comics use the term to describe their own acts during TV meetings, and everyone around the table nods in appreciation and approval. Or are they choking? I can never tell with TV people.

Maybe they're suffocating under a pillow of their own stupidity, since no one really understands the meaning behind political correctness, the arch, high-browed stance it panders to. The phrase was coined as a reaction to racism in the US, to respond with a sort of kindness that had been stifled when hippies disappeared from the US landscape. PC took the place of sympathy which has, since Reaganomics, had a negative, sort of 'girlie' tone to it that few US politicians, especially those who served in 'Nam, can tolerate. Being politically correct makes the user feel more in control and smarter, because they can manipulate a conversation by knowing the proper term to describe, say, an American Indian.

'They're actually indigenous peoples now,' a talk-show host in San Francisco told me while on air recently. 'The word Indian is too marginal.'

'But where are they indigenous to?'

'Well, here of course.'

'They're from San Francisco?'

'No. I mean, yes. My boss' – we were discussing his producer, Sam – 'was born and raised here, but his parents are Cherokee from Kansas. Or was it his grandparents?'

'My grandfather is Italian, from Italy. What does that make me?'

'Good in bed.'

Indigenous, tribal, quasi or semi. All these words are used to describe, politely, 'the truth'. But, strangely enough, the truth is camouflaged. The white user pretends to understand the strife of the minorities, their emotional ups and downs, their need for acceptance and understanding, when all the minorities require is fair pay. I've never met a struggling Costa Rican labourer who was concerned that he be called a 'Latino' as opposed to a 'Hispanic'. He just wants to feed his family. Actually, I've never met a struggling Costa Rican, period. But that's because I'm one of the annoying middle class who keep a distance from anyone who's not like them, but who also has the time and just enough of an education to make up words and worry about who gets called what.

To the targets, the people we're trying to protect – the downtrodden, the homeless, the forgotten – we must appear naïve and bored, like nuns. It's a lesson in tolerance that's become intolerant. As if to say: 'If you don't think this way, if you don't think that a black person from Bristol is better off being called Anglo-African, you're not only wrong, you're evil!' It's pure fascism, plain and simple. It's as if *Guardian* readers had unleashed their consciousness on everybody else, and so it's *naughty* to make jokes about blacks, unless you're black, and *bad* to make fun of fat people, if you're not fat, etc. Suddenly, everyone is tiptoeing around everyone else, frightened they'll be labelled racist because they use the word 'Jew' in a punchline. Or horrified someone will think them misogynist because they think women deal better with stress.

Somehow we've forgotten that it's all in how you say it. To read a brilliant stand-up comic's act is pedantic, but to see it performed is breathtaking. That's because what we say might be clever, but the way we arrange and self-analyse and present is where the fun comes in. Same with all those words we use. They're not 'racist' or 'dangerous' by definition.

Speaking of definitions, let's talk about the word 'gay'. Lots of people I meet are concerned about what I should be called. Is it gay, which pleases the press, or queer, which pleases the hetero hip, since they think gays are trying to reclaim that word? The fact is that all those words are straight-created straight identifiers. Gay is a heterosexual concept. It's a man who looks like a model, dresses like a model and has the brain of a model. He has disposable income, he loves to travel, and he adores – thinks he sometimes is – Madonna. He's a teenage girl really and straights love objectifying him the way they do teenage girls. Or the way they do infants. Try watching a diaper commercial with the sound off. It's like porn. You'll think you're in a bar in Amsterdam.

I'm about as comfortable with the word 'gay' as I am with kiddy porn. I'd prefer to be called a comic. Not a gay comic. Not a queer comic. Not even a gay, queer comic, or a fierce comic, or an alternative comic. It's just the mainstream trying to pigeonhole me, trying to say, OK, he's gay, so it's OK to laugh at his stuff about gays. Which is why, partially, in my act, I make fun of the Holocaust by saying 'Holocaust, schmolocaust, can't they whine about something else?'

The line is meant to be ambiguous, initially. It's meant to start big, and then the actual subject gets small, as I discuss ignorance about the pink triangle as a symbol of oppression, which has since been turned into a fashion accessory. Like the red ribbon, it makes the PC brigade feel like they've done their part to ease hatred in the world by adorning their lapel with a pin. When pressed, they're not even sure what oppression they're curing, or why they should cure oppression, or how they're oppressed.

But if you make fun of that triangle, or this Queen Mum, or that dead Princess, suddenly you're – why mince – I'm the bad guy. I've broken away from the pack. I'm not acting like a good little queer should. I'm not being silent about issues that don't concern a modern gay man, like hair-dos and don'ts. I'm being aggressive, I'm on to. And those straights, those in charge, the folks looking after 'my minority group', don't like rolling over.

Nor are some cocksucking idiots happy about being bottom-feeders either. Which is why I come out against abortion in my act, and in support of the death penalty since, in the US at least, the two go hand in manicured hand. There I go, losing my last supporters: young women and single gay men. How can I say: 'If you wanna talk Holocaust, how about abortion, ladies? 50 million. Can you maybe keep your legs together?'

That is truly evil. No, not really evil. Just wrong. Why? Particularly when I'm only opposed to abortion as a contraceptive device. Who decides what I can and cannot say? Isn't it the people that aren't listening? If I've got a good joke about it, a well-thought-out attack and a point to make, why is it bad? Why is the world dumbing down almost as fast as Woody Allen's films? Why does it bother me? Why not just do my same old weenie jokes, keep playing the clubs and sleep with closeted straight comics? Just doing those three things – particularly the last – would keep me very busy and distracted, which is what 'life' is all about.

But I imagine that when people go for a night out, they wanna see something different. It's a big deal finding a babysitter, getting a cab, grabbing a bite and sitting your tired ass into a pricey seat to hear some faggot rattle on for an hour. So I try to offer them a unique perspective. One that might seem overwrought, desperate, or strangely effortless, but one that might make them look at, say, an Elton John photo just a bit differently next time.

Look, it's not my job to find anyone's comfort zones. I don't give a shit what people like, or think they like, or want to like. I'm not a revolutionary. I'm just a joke writer with an hour to kill, who wants to elevate the level of intelligence in my act to at least that of the audience. If in doing that, I get a beer thrown at me or I lose a 'friend' (read: jealous comic) then so be it. In the meantime, I'll keep fending off my growing array of fans that are sick and tired of being lied to and patronised.

Gosh, get her! I mean me. Get me, sounding all holier than, well, everybody. Strangely enough, the more I find my voice on stage, the more serious comedy becomes for me. Maybe I should go back to telling those 'Americans are so silly' jokes before I lose my mind, and throw all my papers up in the air. ❏

Scott Capurro *is a San Francisco-based stand-up whose performance at the Edinburgh Fringe in August ended in uproar after he 'made jokes' about the Holocaust. His book,* Fowl Play, *was published by Headline in September 1999*

MALACHI O'DOHERTY

Sectarian shenanigans

The best jokes in Northern Ireland are as much about the shame of sectarianism and the easement of guilt as hatred of the other

My brother has a hangover. He says: 'I have a head on me I wouldn't wish on a Protestant.' Everybody laughs. In Catholic Belfast this is a very funny joke, but why? Superficially, the target of the joke is all Protestants, the detestable people on whom all curses – but this hangover – are deserved. Therefore it is a sectarian joke. 'I have a head on me I wouldn't wish on Saddam Hussein, Maggie Thatcher, Ann Widdecombe.' No laughs there.

It appears that the joke is funny because the supposedly detested Protestant is considered in a much more ambiguous way by the joker than more routinely disliked figures. If he had said: 'I have a head on me I wouldn't wish on Tony Blair,' that wouldn't have been funny at all. People are expected to sneer at the prime minister: it is the normal tone in which ordinary people discuss all politicians.

The joke is loaded with the humility of the hangover, the self-deprecation that follows the high night of celebration and foolishness, the instant karma that brings the drunkard down to earth. The real target is the joker himself. He is ashamed and he is sharing his shame. The hung-over, self-deprecating man can admit things about himself that he would not admit at more confident times. One of those things, in this case, is that he is sectarian. His audience laughs, as it would laugh if he exposed any other embarrassment.

But if the joke is about the shame of sectarianism, is it really sectarian at all? In one sense, yes, because it places the Protestant below the teller when he is not hung-over, but above him when he is. The joke says: 'Aren't we real fools being bigots?' And those who agree laugh. Not

Malachi O'Doherty, **In the eye of his beholders.** *Credit: Ian Knox*

to laugh would be to concede that Protestants really are unlikeable people who deserve to be suffering this hangover. Very few people, it seems, really think that. Or it would be to defend Protestants against the jibe.

Some jokes and stories can be interpreted to show up the political advantage that is served by their circulation. Some, unpicked for their secret message, show up a party line, others a secret fear.

There is a modern myth about a joyrider who was captured by the IRA or the Loyalists and who asked if he could take off his new jeans before they kneecapped him. Everybody knows that story. Everybody knows somebody who knows the name of the boy, or of the ambulance driver who brought him in with the neatly folded jeans under his head on the stretcher. The service that myth performs is to ease the guilt of those who make no complaint about the kneecappings, for whatever reason. This story reassures them that a bullet in the leg is not a serious affliction, that reckless young lads think more of their clothes than their flesh anyway.

Another kind of humour is the formal satire on the Troubles, the stuff that is scripted, by comedians like the Hole in the Wall Gang. They 'take the mickey' (and there's a telling phrase) out of themes like 'Love across the Barricades', 'the claims culture' and the smug middle classes who think they live above the conflict, untouched by it. The Gang depicted Sinn Fein at the start of the process as Gerry and the Peacemakers. They have realised there is a deep cynicism about the political machinations of the peace process and that people want to admit, through their laughter, that they understand this – even if they don't want to undo it.

A lot of humour in Northern Ireland serves the desire of people to show that they know what is really going on. For instance: 'Did you hear that Gerry Adams has been turned down for the job of Celtic manager? He couldn't guarantee to stop the beatings.' The beatings the joker is thinking about are the punishment beatings of small-time criminals by the IRA. This is clever. This is knowing. People laugh at it because it is cheeky. It undermines the new respectability of the Republican leader in transition from violence. It says: 'We know all about him, don't we?' But it's not funny.

The Bitter Orange Band has recorded a song, 'The Pope's a darkie'. Again, it is a knowing joke. It doesn't represent actual sectarian bigotry but parodies it. Yet it is a tape that sells to Loyalists in shops that also sell paramilitary gear. Even there, actual unreserved sectarian hatred is mocked and the assumption is that those who listen to the tape want to mock it, though perhaps to assure themselves that their own lesser contempt for Catholics is acceptable.

Some subjects are considered too sacred to be joked about. After the hunger strikes, there were dark jokes about Bobby Sands. One recalled how Elvis, who had died around the same time, arrived in Heaven to be met by Otis Redding. 'We had a party laid on for you, Elvis, but some skinny Irish guy has eaten all the sandwiches.'

This joke is seriously frowned on by Republicans who regard Sands with undiluted reverence. Loyalists don't like it either, because there is something affectionate about it. It depicts Sands as eager and gormless and in Heaven. They prefer to imagine Sands in Hell. Which raises the question: who coined this joke and what interest does it serve? Like the hangover joke, it appears to represent a point of view that is contemptuous of sectarian ardour and wishes to deflate it. It patronises Bobby Sands, but it does not sneer at him.

There is a more vicious sectarian humour that is not funny but expresses the due contempt for the other side in a much more satisfying way for the true bigot than either of those jokes would. 'What is the difference between a Fenian [a Catholic] and an Onion? You don't cry when you slice a Fenian.' The popular sectarian humour is never as brutal as that. Only those who approve indulgent sadism could enjoy that joke. Hard young men might tell it to advertise their brutality, but even they would not laugh spontaneously at it.

It is the truly funny joke that reveals a hidden truth. That truth is often that we are embarrassed by our sectarianism and that we don't take our impassioned political representatives and their traditions as seriously as they think we do. ❏

Malachi O'Doherty is a freelance journalist in Belfast working for the Belfast Telegraph, the Scotsman and the BBC. He is the author of The Trouble With Guns (Blackstaff Press)

FRANÇOIS VINSOT

Laughing in Rwanda

Six years after the genocide, in a street in Kigali, a young girl was huddled on the ground yelling gibberish, throwing dust at passers-by. A crowd gathered and an indignant shopkeeper moved the sick girl out of the way, which only made her yell even louder. A woman passing by relieved the tension by laughing and a few others followed suit. Everybody continued on their way, leaving this bothersome person to whatever her fate might be. I couldn't see the funny side: all I saw was her pain, but then, it was not my story. I suppose I must have missed the point.

I've heard lots of stories told by Rwandans, stories that were horrible, bizarre, often tragic, but I don't remember ever hearing a funny story, nor of any Rwandan comedian.

And then, one evening, the people of Kigali were invited to a show put together by artists from all over Africa. It was devoted to the idea of remembrance and the duty to maintain a written record; and it was, of course, focused on the genocide. Not, on the face of it, the sort of thing to make you split your sides. The text was a montage of testimony by survivors and, from the outset, the audience found it harrowing. It was one of those official functions where it's as important to be seen as it is to watch the show, and it managed to take everyone by surprise.

There were some very explicit scenes of fake violence and accounts of atrocities so minutely detailed that they sounded like messages from beyond the grave. All this was interspersed with pounding musical improvisations, spotlights cutting through the darkness like machine-guns, and presented in a monotone by an old man who seemed to carry the weight of the world on his shoulders. This continued until a character emerged from the audience and interrupted him. He was an imposing, wide-eyed giant of a man who seemed to creep along like a leopard and swallow up all the available space.

To begin with, he spoke like a raving madman, and there were one or two laughs from the audience, then a few more. He stopped dead, stared into the audience, trying to see who it was that had laughed. Then he burst into uncontrollable laughter. It was not the laughter of communication but it carried more significance than any cry; so much so that the other actors gathered round him, waiting to see what he might have to say. The man seemed to grow calmer for a moment. Then he hoisted himself on to a table and said:

'We are all Rwandans on the outside, but they're different outsides, and because we're all coming from all these outsides, we've forgotten where the inside is and we're all going crazy. For example, on the roads, we don't know which side to drive on any more! Those who come from Uganda play it careful and keep to the left, those coming from Burundi play it safe and keep to the right. That kind of madness is really dangerous, yet it would be so simple if everybody were just to drive in the middle of the road!'

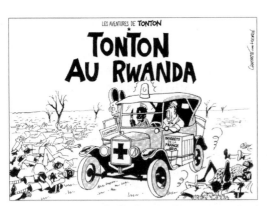

Credit: Courtesy Courrier International

Almost without noticing it, many Rwandans had just heard their first funny story for a long time and they burst into laughter and applause and waved their arms about for joy. The actor continued to act the part of a fool but his words became serious, tragic once more. It was no good, though: the minute he opened his mouth the crowd would laugh and shout things out to him. It had taken a first-class actor from Côte d'Ivoire to dare, after all this time, to make the Rwandans laugh. That laughter still echoes in my memory like some painful surprise. ❑

François Vinsot, a former Africa correspondent for the BBC, is working in the Great Lakes Region for Justice Africa

ROHAN JAYASEKERA

Madness in their method

Performers Jon Hough and David Woods met in 1990 at London's Poor School drama school where they discovered a shared taste for the absurd and madness in their methods over 'midnight beans and toast in David's flat in St Asaph's Road, Brockley'. Today they run Ridiculusmus, one of the least classifiable touring theatre companies around

Madness is a recurring theme in the work of Ridiculusmus. And in the lives of its creators. After the death of Jon's mother in 1982, depression set in, his weight sank to 25 kilos and he was involuntarily 'sectioned' to a stay in south London's Maudsley mental hospital. David was nicknamed 'Mad Dave' at college, having had to come to terms at the age of 13 with the fact that lunacy might be in his genes. Like his grandfather before him, Woods's brother suffers from florid psychosis, or the (allegedly irrational) belief that he has a unique insight on life. Perhaps he does, Jon Hough and David Woods certainly do. They quote Samuel Beckett: 'We are all born mad, some remain so.' Their two-hander about madness and much else besides, *Yes, Yes, Yes*, was a hit at the 1999 Edinburgh Festival. The *Guardian* newspaper's Lyn Gardner said *Yes, Yes, Yes* 'combines first-rate physical skill with such superb comic timing that the descent into mayhem seems quite logical [where] optimism is a complete madness in the face of reality'.

Yes, Yes, Yes was deeply influenced by a trip to India in 1996 and an encounter with scooter-riding Swami Parmananda and his island community of orphans, homeless and happily ranting mental patients. Later, in Bangalore, they ran into YMN Murthy, ex-textiles worker and founder of the International Humour Society, who teaches that laughing brings you closer to God.

Ridiculusmus began performing to the mentally ill in 1993, bringing a production of *Three Men in a Boat* to a group of Craigmillar adults with learning difficulties. They were then invited to play Craig Dunain psychiatric hospital, Inverness, beginning a regular partnership. During a perfomance at Craig Dunain, David, in character, prepared a fried egg. 'But not knowing how to cook, he neglects to use a cooker and offers a raw runny mess to J. [Jon] declines and he offers it to the audience. Eager audience member greedily gulps it down.'

They run the same performances for both the mentally ill and the nominally 'normal', whom they like to diagnose as mad, but showing 'normality traits'. Sometimes they are invited to work with specific groups, such as David's ten-week residency with an adult epilepsy society in Croydon, and Jon's work at Gransha secure unit in Derry, but the work remains the same with all. 'We dangle professional actors out of windows by their ankles when they attend audition workshops and we do the same to adults with learning difficulties. We always get into more trouble with the former!'

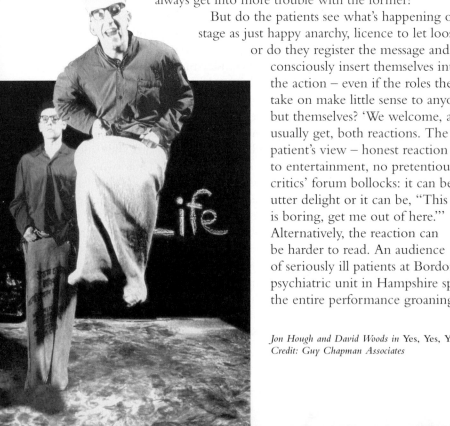

But do the patients see what's happening on stage as just happy anarchy, licence to let loose, or do they register the message and consciously insert themselves into the action – even if the roles they take on make little sense to anyone but themselves? 'We welcome, and usually get, both reactions. The patient's view – honest reaction to entertainment, no pretentious critics' forum bollocks: it can be utter delight or it can be, "This is boring, get me out of here."' Alternatively, the reaction can be harder to read. An audience of seriously ill patients at Bordon psychiatric unit in Hampshire spent the entire performance groaning

Jon Hough and David Woods in Yes, Yes, Yes. *Credit: Guy Chapman Associates*

Jon Hough and David Woods in Yes,
Yes, Yes. *The words chalked in the*
background read 'Truth, Life'.
Credit: Guy Chapman Associates

and moaning throughout. There was no apparent concentration or focus
on the piece. 'Afterwards the carers said, "They were really gripped,
what you did was amazing."'

Not all get the point. During one performance one carer mistakenly
believed that some inoffensive semi-nudity was about to turn into
stark nakedness. She 'ordered her charges, who comprised 90% of
the audience, to leave the theatre. This revealed more about her own
inhibitions than theirs. It doesn't happen often. Usually we are re-
booked everywhere. Promoters like the idea of being on the edge
without being directly responsible for the trip there.'

Ridiculusmus has no expectations of its audiences, makes no
demands. 'They come in, listen, open their hearts, play. They go out,
think, ponder, change.' David's mentally ill brother felt able to come off
his drugs after seeing the duo's shows in Edinburgh. 'There haven't been
any noticeable side effects,' he told David after time. 'Yes, there have,'
David replied. 'You are back.' ❑

Ridiculusmus performs Yes, Yes, Yes *at the Village Hall, Dilton March, near*
Bath, on 28 November and across England and Wales during December. Check
their website www.ridiculu.dircon.co.uk for dates and locations
RJ

MONTY PYTHON'S FLYING CIRCUS

The funniest joke in the world

VOICE-OVER This man is Ernest Scribbler ... writer of jokes. In a few moments, he will have written the funniest joke in the world ... and, as a consequence, he will die ... laughing.

The writer stops writing, pauses to look at what he has written ... a smile spreads across his face, turning very, very slowly to uncontrolled hysterical laughter ... he staggers to his feet and reels across the room, helpless with mounting mirth and eventually collapses and dies on the floor.

VOICE-OVER It was obvious that this joke was lethal ... no one could read it and live ...

The scribbler's mother enters. She sees him dead, she gives a little cry of horror and bends over his body, weeping. Broken, she notices the piece of paper in his hand and (thinking it is a suicide note – for he has not been doing very well for the last 13 years) picks it up and reads it in between sobs. Immediately she breaks out into hysterical laughter, leaps three feet into the air and falls down dead without more ado. Cut to news-type shot of commentator standing in front of the house.

COMMENTATOR (*reverentially*) This morning, shortly after 11 o'clock, comedy struck this little house in Dibley Road. Sudden ... violent ... comedy. Police have sealed off the area, and Scotland Yard's crack inspector is with me now.

INSPECTOR I shall enter the house and attempt to remove the joke.

At this point an upstairs window in the house is flung open and a doctor, with stethoscope, rears his head out hysterical with laughter, and dies hanging over the windowsill. The commentator and the inspector look up briefly and sadly, and then continue as if they are used to such sights this morning.

INSPECTOR I shall be aided by the sound of sombre music, played on gramophone records, and also by the chanting of laments by the men of

Q Division ... (*He indicates a little knot of dour-looking policemen standing nearby.*) The atmosphere thus created should protect me in the eventuality of me reading the joke.

He gives a signal. The group of policemen start groaning and chanting biblical laments. 'The Dead March' is heard. The inspector squares his shoulders and bravely starts walking into the house.

COMMENTATOR There goes a brave man. Whether he comes out alive or not, this will surely be remembered as one of the most courageous and gallant acts in police history.

The inspector suddenly appears at the door, helpless with laughter, holding the joke aloft. He collapses and dies. Cut to stock film of army vans driving along dark roads.

VOICE-OVER It was not long before the Army became interested in the military potential of the killer joke ... Top brass were impressed. Tests on Salisbury Plain confirmed the joke's devastating effectiveness at a range of up to 50 yards.

Cut to shot looking out of slit in pillbox. Zoom through slit to distance where a solitary figure is standing on the windswept plain. He is a bespectacled, weedy lance corporal looking cold and miserable. Pan across to 50 yards away where two helmeted soldiers are at their positions beside a blackboard on an easel covered with a cloth. Cut in to corporal's face – registering complete lack of comprehension as well as stupidity. Man on top of pillbox waves flag. The soldiers reveal the joke to the corporal. He peers at it, thinks about the meaning, sniggers, and dies. Two watching generals are very impressed.

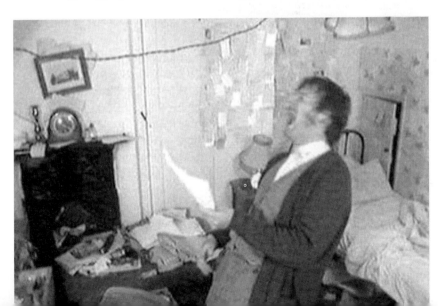

GENERALS Fantastic!

Cut to colonel talking to camera.

COLONEL All through the winter of '43 we had translators working, in joke-proof conditions, to try and produce a German version of the joke. They worked on one word each for greater safety. One of them saw two words of the joke and spent several weeks in hospital. But apart from that, things went pretty quickly, and we soon had the joke by January, in a form which our troops couldn't understand, but which the Germans could.

Cut to a trench in the Ardennes. Members of the joke brigade are crouched holding pieces of paper with the joke on them.

VOICE-OVER So, on July 8th 1944, the joke was first told to the enemy in the Ardennes ...

COMMANDING NCO Tell the ... joke.

JOKE BRIGADE (*together*) Wenn ist das Nunstück git und Slotermeyer? Ja! ... Beiherhund das Oder die Flipperwaldt gersput!

Pan out of the British trench across war-torn landscape and come to rest where presumably the German trench is. There is a pause and then a knot of Germans rear up in hysterics.

VOICE-OVER It was a fantastic success. Over 60,000 times as powerful as Britain's great pre-war joke ...

Stock film of Chamberlain brandishing the 'Peace in our time' bit of paper.

VOICE-OVER ... and one which Hitler just couldn't match.

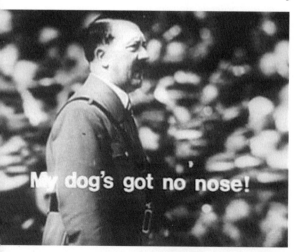

Film of Hitler rally. Hitler speaks; subtitles are superimposed.

SUBTITLE 'My dog's got no nose.'

A young person responds:

SUBTITLE 'How does he smell?'

Hitler speaks:

SUBTITLE 'Awful.'

VOICE-OVER In action it was deadly ... The German casualties were appalling.

Cut to a German hospital and a ward full of casualties still

laughing hysterically. Cut to Nazi interrogation room. An officer from the joke brigade has a light shining in his face. A Gestapo officer is interrogating him; another (clearly labelled 'Gestapo Officer') stands behind him.

NAZI Vott is the big joke?

OFFICER I can only give you name, rank and why did the chicken cross the road?

NAZI That's not funny! (*Slaps him.*) I vant to know the joke ...

OFFICER I can stand physical pain, you know.

NAZI Ah ... you're no fun. All right, Otto.

Otto starts tickling the officer who starts laughing.

OFFICER Oh no – anything but that please no, all right I'll tell you.
They stop.

NAZI Quick, Otto. The typewriter.

Otto goes over to the typewriter and they wait expectantly. The officer produces a piece of paper out of his breast pocket and reads.

OFFICER Wenn ist das Nunstück git und Slotermeyer? Ja! ... Beiherhund das Oder die Flipperwaldt gersput!

Otto at the typewriter explodes with laughter and dies.

NAZI Ach! Zat iss not funny!

> *Bursts into laughter and dies. A guard bursts in with machine-gun. The British officer leaps on the table.*

OFFICER (*lightning speed*) Wenn ist das Nunstück git und Slotermeyer? Ja! ... Beiherhund das Oder die Flipperwaldt gersput!

> *The guard reels back and collapses laughing. British officer makes his escape. Cut to stock film of German scientists working in laboratories.*

VOICE-OVER But at Peenemunde in the autumn of '44, the Germans were working on a joke of their own ... by December their joke was ready, and Hitler gave the order for the V-Joke to be broadcast in English.

> *Cut to 1940s wartime radio set with couple anxiously listening to it.*

RADIO (*crackly German voice*) Der ver zwei peanuts, valking down der strasse, and von vas ... assaulted! Peanut. Ho-ho-ho-ho.

> *Radio bursts into 'Deutschland Uber Alles'. The couple look at each other and then in blank amazement at the radio. Cut to modern BBC2 interview. The commentator in a woodland glade.*

COMMENTATOR In 1945 Peace broke out. It was the end of the Joke. Joke warfare was banned at a special session of the Geneva Convention, and in 1950 the last remaining copy of the joke was laid to rest here in the Berkshire countryside, never to be told again.

> *He walks away revealing a monument on which is written: 'To the unknown Joke'.* ❏

From Monty Python's Flying Circus, *series one, episode one, titled 'Whither Canada', first shown on 5 October 1969*

Credit for all photographs: Courtesy Python (Monty) Productions

NILOU MOBASSER

Crocodile smile

Humour has no immunity from prosecution as far as the opponents of free expression in Iran are concerned. Cartoonist **Nik-Ahang Kowsar** was arrested earlier this year for drawing a crocodile weeping copiously over the way he is being mistreated by a 'dissident journalist'. The word crocodile (*temsah*) was deemed to have been too close to the name of a well-known hardline cleric – Mesbah – and the country was plunged into days of 'crocodile' rage and demonstrations by the usual 'defenders of values'.

The satirist **Ebrahim Nabavi** has been forced to find sources of inspiration in Tehran's Evin Prison since his detention in August, on occasion in solitary confinement (Index Index p117). But the joke goes on: those few remaining pro-freedom papers continue to present their cartoon offerings on their own state. No more crocodiles, but the conservative press is biting back: reformist journalists are depicted as lackeys of Uncle Sam. Enough. Let the press speak. ❏

Nilou Mobasser is a writer and translator working for the BBC

Nik-Ahang Kowsar counts the days. Credit for all cartoons: Courtesy Asr e Azedegan, *Iran*

Films

&

fun

*Without humour, you cannot run a
sweetie-shop, let alone a nation*
John Buchan

JULIAN PETLEY

Laughs and sneezes

'Comedy is less likely than tragedy to omit to take human suffering seriously enough' *Bertolt Brecht*

In 1941, Bertolt Brecht wrote *The Resistible Rise of Arturo Ui*, in which he recast Hitler's career in terms of a Chicago gangster's takeover of the city's greengrocery market. He himself described it as a 'parable play, written with the aim of destroying the dangerous respect commonly felt for great killers', an enterprise in which ridicule played a key role.

Brecht's favourite screen actor was Charlie Chaplin, and the way in which Brecht used humour to undercut Nazi pretension and pomposity clearly echoed Chaplin's *The Great Dictator*, released the previous year to great acclaim.

In *The Great Dictator*, Chaplin plays Adenoid Hynkel, Dictator of Tomania (as in ptomaine poisoning), and also, in a nicely subversive touch, a Jewish barber who is Hynkel's/Hitler's double. Mussolini becomes Benzini Napaloni, Dictator of Bacteria, with Goering satirised as Herring and Goebbels as Garbitsch. Tomania's symbol is the double cross and its leader is referred to as the 'Fooey'.

Such humour may come across today as a mite childish, but this mere name-calling is put in the shade by the way in which the film fatally pricks and deflates Nazi rhetoric by other, more effective means. For example, Hynkel's speeches, which are guttural gibberish from the start, rapidly degenerate into mere coughs and splutters, and their source is all too clearly hinted at when Hynkel, after a particularly heated climax, deliberately pours a glass of water into the crotch of his trousers. Meanwhile, the absurd vanity of the *Führerprinzip* is parodied by the way in which Hynkel dashes off to be painted and sculpted whenever he has

The Great Dictator, *1940: Adenoid Hynkel and Benzini Napaloni in culinary rivalry.*
Credit: © Roy Export Company Establishment

a few spare seconds; by the lackey whose job it is to put out his tongue so that Hynkel can pass the flap of an envelope across it to seal his letters; by Hynkel's famous dance with the globe, which ends on a note of complete bathos as it bursts in his face; and by his increasingly frenzied (and thwarted) attempts to arrange the mise-en-scène of his palatial apartments so that he is always at a physical advantage beside the rather more substantial Napaloni.

At the end of *The Great Dictator* – in which, by a series of mix-ups, it is the little Jewish barber and not Hynkel who annexes Osterlich and

To Be or Not to Be, 1942: theatrical putsch

finds himself expected to deliver a speech to his new subjects – Chaplin steps out of character to make a deadly serious and passionately anti-Nazi speech that is addressed primarily to the film audience itself. Such overt didacticism was unusual in Hollywood films of the time; indeed, it still comes across as somewhat startling and even puts one in mind of Brecht's famed 'distanciation' devices. None the less, today's audiences may well find that it is the film's iconoclastic and irreverent sense of humour, rather than Chaplin's overt sentiments, however noble, well-meaning and strikingly expressed, that is its most devastating anti-Nazi weapon.

Distanciation, albeit of a kind at once more subtle and more thoroughgoing, is also the hallmark of an anti-Nazi comedy that was poorly received at the time but whose reputation now outshines Chaplin's film: Ernst Lubitsch's *To Be or Not to Be* (1942). This is set in Warsaw around the German invasion of Poland and focuses on the frantic efforts of a Polish theatre troupe, led by Josef Tura (Jack Benny) and his wife Maria (Carole Lombard), to stop the Polish spy Professor Siletsky betraying the Polish underground to the head of the Gestapo in Warsaw, Colonel Ehrhardt.

Lubitsch himself, in an article in the *New York Times*, summed up the charges laid against his film: 'I am accused of three major sins – of having violated every traditional form in mixing melodrama with comedy-satire or even farce, of endangering our war effort in treating the Nazi menace too lightly, and of exhibiting extremely bad taste in having chosen present-day Warsaw as a background for comedy.' In answering the first criticism, Lubitsch stated: 'I was tired of the two established, recognised recipes: drama with comedy relief, and comedy with drama relief. I made up my mind to make a picture with no attempt to relieve anybody from anything at any time.' As for the other charges, Lubitsch argued that he had deliberately avoided 'the methods usually employed in pictures, novels and plays to signify Nazi terror. No actual torture chamber is photographed, no flogging is shown, no close-up of excited Nazis using their whips and rolling their eyes in lust. My Nazis are different: they passed that stage long ago.' Against such Nazis, Lubitsch judged, ridicule was the best weapon. In this, he was echoed by Melchior Lengyel, one of the film's scriptwriters, who argued that since 'Nazis and fascists are essentially humourless creatures' it was better to use humour against them rather than 'put wind into their sails by saturating the public with the impression of their power and invincibility'.

The success of this strategy is abundantly evident from the film's opening scenes. In the first, a seemingly bemused Hitler stands in a Warsaw street outside Maslowski's delicatessen, surrounded by curious crowds but quite bereft of his usual awe-inspiring entourage. In the second, in what appears to be the offices of the Gestapo, an officer yawns while giving his adjutant the Heil Hitler salute, and the adjutant later uses the same salute to interrupt and bring to a premature close an increasingly tricky interrogation about an anti-Hitler joke which he has just told. Finally, after an absurdly exaggerated fusillade of off-screen Heil Hitlers, the Führer himself enters the room, only to return the Heil Hitler salutes from the assembled company with the words 'Heil Myself!'

At this point, in one of the cinema's great moments, the words 'that's not in the script!' ring out, and the whole scene is suddenly and stunningly revealed to be a rehearsal by Tura's company of the play *Gestapo*. The words are those of the play's furious director Dobosh, and 'Hitler' is the bit-part player Bronski, who replies that his ad-lib will get a laugh. In this he's backed up by the humble spear-carrier Greenberg, who argues that 'a laugh is nothing to be sneezed at'. None the less, Dobosh insists that *Gestapo* is 'a serious play, a realistic drama, a document of Nazi Germany' and tells Bronski that his Hitler isn't realistic, complaining that 'to me he's just a man with a little moustache', to which the make-up man retorts, 'But so is Hitler.' The first scene is then revealed to be a rare example of the flash-forward, as Bronski walks out on to the street to prove that his Hitler is indeed convincing. Sure enough, everyone is taken in – except for a little girl who shyly steps forward to ask 'Mr Bronski' to give her his autograph!

Clearly, after Dobosh's shattering eruption into this scene, much of its meaning is actually carried by the dialogue. But by plunging us so abruptly into the illusion–reality dichotomy, Lubitsch makes it impossible for us to take anything that follows at its face value, and in the rest of the film it is the dazzlingly theatrical mise-en-scène that gives the film its vertiginously self-reflexive quality. As Graham Petrie put it in *Film Comment* in 1974: 'People will seldom be exactly what they appear to be, or present themselves as being; events that look staged and phoney may turn out to be part of the pattern of normal life, while the most

The Producers, *1968: demystifying fascism. Credit: Canal +*

apparently realistic incidents will be part of a stage performance or a conscious act of deception.'

In particular, the real Nazis turn out to be as bogus and caricatured as their stage counterparts, as in the scenes in which Tura impersonates Ehrhardt without ever having encountered him, only to discover later, when they do actually meet (by which time Tura is impersonating Siletsky), that life does indeed imitate art. It is in these scenes that the subversive humour of *To Be or Not to Be* reaches its zenith. Not content with simply satirising the bloated pomp of Nazi displays of power, the film's remarkable mise-en-scène cumulatively reveals the entire Nazi political machine to be little more than an unpleasantly bombastic and bullying form of theatre and its leader simply a ham actor.

Mel Brooks's *The Producers* (1968) is equally resolute in its refusal to take Nazi rhetoric at its own inflated face value. (It's no coincidence that Brooks remade *To Be or Not to Be* in 1983.) In this respect the film's most subversive scene is not the famous 'Springtime for Hitler and Germany' but the casting call for Hitler, which opens with the immortal lines, 'Will the dancing Hitlers please wait in the wings. We're only seeing singing Hitlers.' There then follows an increasingly bizarre series of would-be Hitlers singing 'A Wandering Ministrel I', 'Have You Heard the German Band' and 'Beautiful Dreamer', until the producers finally alight upon the abomination of acid-casualty Lorenzo St Dubois (LSD), who will later bring the house down with his bluesy rendition of 'Gonna crush Poland, and then I'm gonna take over France'. If there's any truly effective antidote to what Walter Benjamin called fascism's 'aestheticisation of politics' and Susan Sontag the 'fascination of fascism' (both so seductively exploited by Leni Riefenstahl in her films) then this, surely, is it. ❏

Julian Petley is a writer and film critic. He teaches at Brunel University, UK

The troubled life of Brian

Monty Python's Life of Brian: *the scene that troubled the censors.*
Credit: Courtesy Python (Monty) Productions

Filmed in autumn 1978, *Monty Python's Life of Brian* – a skit on the life of Christ – was in trouble even before it hit the screen. EMI cancelled production fearing a blasphemy charge, leaving George Harrison to rescue the film. Before the British Board of Film Censors [BBFC] finally allowed it to open uncut in August 1979, organisations like the Festival of Light and Citizens against Blasphemy were condemning it or threatening prosecution. Predictably, the Catholic Church put it on its Index of banned works: to watch it was a sin.

Though rated '14' in Britain, *Monty Python's Life of Brian* was given an 'X' certificate – adults only – in some areas of the country and others banned it completely: it took Swansea District Council in Wales until 1997 to lift its ban. In the US, the film was given an R – over 18 – rating; Norway banned it as blasphemous until 1980; Sweden marketed the film as 'so funny it was banned in Norway!' ❏

JSR

FLASHPOINTS

Media on trial

The joy of spontaneous revolutions, such as the one that shook the Milosevic regime out of its tree in October, is that they give both actors and audience a shorthand for closure and a foretaste of spring, with its promise of renewal and a million Internet start-ups. But beneath the smoke, the laughter and the carnival two-step of defecting flunkies, the machinery of power is still audible as screens and trapdoors slide open, and bad reputations hurtle through fire-doors and run for the exits.

That such revolutions are carried out by a generation impatient of the obsessions of the past means they entail a degree of wilful forgetfulness and a collective commitment to self-conscious reinvention. This is not a bad thing for the peoples of the former Yugoslavia if it comes right, but the mass killings and casual brutality which have characterised more than a decade of Serbia's national life must not be permitted to slip down the drains of a smug, generational amnesia. The 'new' Serbia is still the old Serbia, its face momentarily illuminated by the relief of having, at last, rid itself of Milosevic.

It is not the task of this column to second-guess the juridical calculus of atonement and penitence that faces President Vojislav Kostunica and his people as they set course for a new Serbian role in the region and in Europe. But it is relevant to speculate on the possible fate of the state-controlled press and electronic media that were so central in ensuring that Milosevic's preferred version of the news was the one most Serbians always saw and read, and of their editors and journalists, who benefited financially from their intimate relationship with power. Spomenka Jovic, a chief editor with Radio-Television Serbia (RTS), was given the right to buy a spacious Belgrade apartment on a US$37-per-year mortgage for services to the Socialist Party. It was not surprising that RTS was the demonstrators' second target, after the invasion of Parliament on 5 October.

The first indication that Milosevic was tottering triggered a wave of editorial mutinies in the state media, but it would be rash to attribute them to sudden conversions to press freedom values. On 1 and 2 October Radio Obrenovac, Radio Smederevo, Radio Novi Becej, Radio Zajecar, Radio Lazarevac, Radio Mladenovac and Radio Sremcic refused to rebroadcast RTS news and 90 staff from Studio B announced their intention to go on strike if they were not allowed to report freely on the elections and their aftermath. On the same day, 56 journalists at *Politika*, Serbia's oldest newspaper and the regime's closest print ally, signed a petition demanding 'democratisation'. On 5 October, editor Dragan Hadzi Antic – who once stepped out with Milosevic's daughter – slipped out the back way as Belgraders queued to buy the morning edition with its collectable headline 'Democracy Comes to Serbia'. Days earlier, the front page was devoted to a Chinese analysis of the 'ruthless interference of the West'.

The first sign that President Vojislav Kostunica would take a more liberal line with the press was his personal pardon on 10 October of Kraljevo journalist Miroslav Filipovic, who was jailed on 26 July for espionage and disseminating false information (*Index* 4/2000, 5/2000), charges which still stand. On his release from Nis Military Prison, he said: 'I spent five months inside for no reason, but that is the fate of journalists in our country, although that time is past now.'

But is it? Calls for the repeal of the Public Information Act of October 1998 have gone unheeded. This pernicious law plundered hundreds of thousands of dollars in fines from the small independent media sector as well as individual journalists. On 12 October, the Association of Independent News Media (ANEM) called for a reassessment on the way in which radio and TV frequency licences had been allocated, usually on the grounds of commercial cronyism. And, despite an apparent privatisation programme last summer, the state continues to own 50% of *Politika*, while the balance is held by Milosevic's associates, Ljuba Mihailovic and Dragan Tomic. While the legal and financial apparatus of Milosevic's cowed and compliant media continues to exist, so does the possibility of counter-revolution. What is required is complete discovery and disinvestment of party interest in the Serbian media.

And what of the journalists and editors who colluded with the regime? ANEM director Veran Matic told *Index*:

'I think that a thorough investigation should be done and the truth should be ascertained. This is not revenge. Journalists who spread hatred certainly shouldn't be permitted to do their job any more. Journalists, like judges, lawyers and doctors, are members of a so-called ethical profession. It is impossible to imagine that a doctor who, unconsciously or on purpose, kills the patient should be allowed to practise medicine in the future.'

And if you want a reminder of just how the Milosevic era still lingers in the ozone, visit www.serbia-info.com. Would someone at the ministry please change the content? Please? ❏

MG & LF

A censorship chronicle incorporating information from the American Association for the Advancement of Science Human Rights Action Network (AAASHRAN), Amnesty International (AI), Article 19 (A19), Alliance of Independent Journalists (AJI), the BBC Monitoring Service Summary of World Broadcasts (SWB), Centre for Journalism in Extreme Situations (CJES), the Committee to Protect Journalists (CPJ), Canadian Journalists for Free Expression (CJFE), Glasnost Defence Foundation (GDF), Information Centre of Human Rights & Democracy Movements in China (ICHRDMC), Instituto de Prensa y Sociedad (IPYS), The UN's Integrated Regional Information Network (IRIN), the Inter-American Press Association (IAPA), the International Federation of Journalists (IFJ/FIP), Human Rights Watch (HRW), the Media Institute of Southern Africa (MISA), Network for the Defence of Independent Media in Africa (NDIMA), International PEN (PEN), Open Media Research Institute (OMRI), Pacific Islands News Association (PINA), Radio Free Europe/Radio Liberty (RFE/RL), Reporters Sans Frontières (RSF), the World Association of Community Broadcasters (AMARC), World Association of Newspapers (WAN), the World Organisation Against Torture (OMCT) and other sources

ALGERIA

On 22 August it was reported that **El Kadi Ihsane**, previously editor of *La Tribune* and now an independent journalist, was detained by police while travelling to Tunisia for a family holiday. Ihsane was arrested in similar circumstances in 1998 when he was stopped at Algiers airport en route to a conference in Geneva (*Index* 4/1998). (IFJ)

ANGOLA

On 8 August, journalist **Rafael Marques** was refused the right to travel to the US, where he was to have received a prize. Marques is presently serving a six-month suspended sentence for defamation of President José Eduardo dos Santos (*Index* 1/2000, 2/2000, 3/2000. (RSF)

The government has proposed new legislation under which journalists could be charged for publishing, disseminating or reproducing news that 'attacks the honour and reputation of the president'. If passed, the law will make it practically impossible for journalists to cover any matter relating to the country's political life without risking incarceration. (RSF, CPJ)

ARGENTINA

Press photographer **Jorge Larrosa** of Buenos Aires daily *Página 12* received threatening phone calls in August over pictures he took implicating police officers in an attack on the National Bank on 17 September 1999. The photographs are being used as evidence in a judicial investigation. (RSF)

AUSTRIA

The far-right Freedom Party politician **Jörg Haider** lost a libel battle against *Kurier* newspaper on 26 September. Haider took the best-selling journal to court after it criticised his refer-ence to Nazi concentration camps as 'punishment centres', an expression which he insisted was 'an unmistakable term of reference which was correct and proper'. This argument was thrown out by Judge Bruno Weis who held: 'The term punishment centre comes from a single document from the Third Reich in 1941 which referred to mass extermination camps as punishment centres. That is the only place the term has come from.' (*Daily Telegraph*)

AZERBAIJAN

On 11 August police and local officials resorted to insults and violence to prevent six independent journalists from entering a camp for displaced persons in the Sabirabad region. (Turan, RFE/RL)

On 18 August a Baku court granted permission to ban the printing and distribution of the independent tri-weekly *Uch Noqte* (*Index* 5/2000). The court's decision was reportedly based on a new law, adopted on 13 February of this year, which stipulates that a media outlet that loses three lawsuits within 12 months can be shut down. However, *Uch Noqte* has lost only one case since the law came into effect. (CPJ)

Gunduz Tahirli, editor of the leading independent daily *Azadlyg*, was questioned for over three hours at the prosecutor general's office on 5 September. He was asked to sign an affidavit promising not to disclose detailed information about the interview. On his release, Tahirli could only say that his visit to the office was connected to the 29 August arrest of editor **Rauf Arifoglu** on charges of attempted hijacking. (CPJ)

On 5 October **Faiq Zulfugarov**, president of the independent television station ABA, announced that the government was shutting down the station, although official papers had yet to be submitted. Zulfugarov believed that Ali Hassanov, head of the president's 'socio-polit-ical division', ordered the closure after he rejected offers to put the station under the government's unofficial control. (JuHI)

Rauf Arifoglu, editor of leading opposition daily *Yeni Musavet*, was released from solitary confine-ment on 6 October after six weeks of imprisonment. Arifoglu was charged on 29 August with partic-ipation in an attempted plane hijacking, terrorism and posses-sion of illegal weapons. A charge of calling for a *coup d'état* was later pressed against him. The charges result from an attempted airplane hijacking on 18 August in the Azeri enclave of Nakhchivan when the hijacker, a member of opposition party Musavat, telephoned Arifoglu and asked him to publish his demands in *Yeni Musavat*. (CPJ, JuHI, CJES, A19, RFE/RL, RSF)

BANGLADESH

On 25 August **Farazi Ajmol Hossain**, a senior reporter with the daily *Ittefaq* and secretary of the Jessore press club, received death threats by telephone. A shroud was sent to his home with a letter threatening to kill him. (RSF)

Shaharier Kabir, a freelance journalist columnist, was stabbed in the face and arm on 28 August by four unidentified men. He was on his way home from a meeting at Dhaka University when the men stopped him on his motorcycle and asked him to go with them. When Kabir screamed for help, the men stabbed him before running off. (RSF)

Journalists reporting on the dis-appearance of Nurul Islam, a leader of the opposition Bangladesh Nationalist Party, have been subject to attacks by the Lakhipur authorities. *Dainik Manabzamin* reporter **Sheikh Mamunur Rashid** received death threats on 4 October while searching for information on the case. The hotel he was staying in was raided by police and municipality workers who threat-ened him with 'reprisals'. On 6 October, journalist **Ekramul Haq Bulbul** from *Dainik Prothom Alo*, who had been investigating the involvement of the Lakhipur mayor in the case, was forced to flee after he was attacked by armed men. The mayor, Abu Taher, threatened to 'break the limbs' of journalists trying to implicate him and warned reporters to 'leave the town or face very dire consequences'. (RSF)

BELARUS

More than 100,000 copies of a special edition of the Minsk-based independent weekly *Rabochy* (Worker), the newspaper of the Belarusian Free Trade Union, were confiscated by police on 13 September because it urged readers to participate in the

'Boycott-2000' campaign org-anised by the opposition prior to the 15 October elec-tions. The newspaper's founder and editor, **Vitar Ivashkevich**, was arrested along with the lawyer **Dzmitry Kastiukevich** and **Yury Budzko**, the general director of Magic publishing house which printed the weekly. They were charged with 'propa-gandising' an electoral boycott. The court ruled at the trial on 18 September that the confisca-tion of *Robochy* was legal. (CPJ)

Alyaksandr Kadukou, a student at the Belarus State University, was fined by a Minsk Court on 4 September for distributing leaflets calling for the boycott of the 15 October legislative polls despite the fact that the Electoral Code does not prohibit campaigning for an election boycott. (RFE/RL)

Secret service agents detained a foreign citizen on 16 September on charges on espionage, but they refuse to disclose his name, profession or nationality even though he faces up to 15 years' imprisonment. According to the KGB, the foreigner had allegedly lured citizens to collect infor-mation, coordinated a local agents network and supplied them with spy equipment and cash. It is believed that the detainee might be a foreign embassy worker without diplomatic immunity, or a foreign businessman. (Radio Racyja)

BOSNIA-HERZEGOVINA

On 19 August High Represent-ative Wolfgang Petritsch ordered Radio Yugoslavia to stop broadcasting from a transmitting centre near Bijeljina within 48 hours. The order, signed by the representative of the Bosnian Federation Independent Media Commission and the Prime Minister of the Republika Srpska, Milorad Dodik, was criticised by many senior officials. (ANEM)

BRAZIL

Justice Minister José Gregori has imposed strict restrictions on the broadcasting of sex and violence on television. TV stations were given a week to comply with the new ratings system introduced in September, which tries to protect children and teenagers from adult-content programming. Although criticised by some media as censorship, the policy has received the support of children's rights groups. (IPS)

BRITAIN

On 15 September the British Board of Film Classification finally allowed *Deep Throat*, one of the world's most notorious sex films, to be seen in its uncut format. The 1972 film caused outrage when it was released and is widely credited with breaking down US censorship laws. The Board also passed another infamous movie, *Debbie Does Dallas*, for viewing without any cuts. (*The Times*)

Names and addresses of known paedophiles will not be made public knowledge under new measures to protect children from sex offenders. A 'Sarah's Law', named after recent child murder victim Sarah Payne (*Index* 5/2000), would have allowed

parents to find out the whereabouts of all known child molesters in their district. But the legislation was dismissed on 16 September by Home Secretary Jack Straw as impracticable. (*Guardian*)

Defence Secretary Geoff Hoon obtained a court order against the Northern Ireland edition of the *Sunday People* to stop it from publishing details of allegations of security force collusion with paramilitaries. In one story the tabloid alleged that a top army officer had ordered the murder of a Catholic pensioner to protect an informer in the IRA. The paper went to the High Court to fight the gagging order for the second time on 29 September but failed to overrule it. (BBC)

Seven-year-old Catholic Katicha Morgan was banned from wearing a silver crucifix by her Church of England school, it was reported on 4 October. The school denied there was religious discrimination in the ban, stating that jewellery was prohibited out of a consideration for safety. (*Daily Telegraph*)

A judge ruled on 6 October that *Punch* magazine was guilty of contempt for publishing an article in July by former M15 agent **David Shayler** (*Index* 3/2000, 5/2000). The article about an IRA bombing campaign apparently breached an often ignored 1997 injunction barring newspapers from publishing information disclosed by Shayler. The judge admitted to finding no evidence to suggest that the article posed a threat to national security. *Punch* was found guilty of

'undermining the administration of justice'. (*Guardian*)

The BBC's *Panorama* programme won a court battle to be allowed to air its programme revealing the names of the suspects behind the 1998 bomb attack in Omagh. Lawyers for the Northern Ireland Human Rights Commission applied to the High Court in Belfast for an injunction on the grounds that it could prejudice any subsequent trial. The judge, Mr Justice Kerr, announced that the programme could be aired only 90 minutes before it was scheduled to start on 9 October. (*Daily Telegraph, Guardian*)

BURMA

Cheng Poh, a 77-year-old lawyer, was sentenced on 14 September on charges of distributing foreign news articles. He will serve two consecutive seven-year prison terms in Rangoon's Insein Prison for allegedly violating the 1950 Emergency Provisions Act and the 1962 Printers and Publishers Registration Law. It has been reported that the authorities will not transfer him to a prison hospital although he is quite weak. (CPJ)

James Mawdsley (*Index* 6/1999, 1/2000), a British pro-democracy campaigner jailed last year for possessing anti-regime pamphlets, has declared that he was beaten on 28 September by prison guards. While the government strongly denied this, attesting that the wounds were 'self-inflicted', it was reported on 16 October that Mawdsley would be 'sent home' to Britain 'within days'. Mawdsley, who was held in Keng Tung jail, was allegedly attacked by 15 guards, resulting in two black eyes, a broken nose and fears that 'irreparable damage may have been done to his internal organs'. (Yahoo! Asia)

CANADA

Michel Auger, a veteran crime reporter with the Québec French-language daily *Le Journal de Montréal*, was shot five times by an unidentified gunman while parking at the newspaper's offices on 13 September. Auger, who kept his telephone number and address private and took a different route to work every day, managed to call an ambulance after being shot and had surgery which saved his life. The attack came the day after his latest article on organised crime in the province was published, including shots of local mafia and Hell's Angels gangsters. (CJFE)

CHINA

Falun Gong adherents continue to fall foul of the authorities in numbers too great to record here in detail. For fully referenced information about victims of the persecution from 7 August to 7 October, please visit: www.indexoncensorship.org/news/

Jiang Shihua, a teacher from Sichuan Province, was arrested on 18 August having posted articles critical of the government on the Internet from his own Internet café. He was charged with 'incitement to subvert state power' and faces a possible ten years in prison. The journalist **Qi Yanchen** (*Index* 4/2000) was

sentenced to four years in prison on 19 September in Hebei Province. He was arrested in September last year on charges of subversion relating to articles published in Hong Kong and on the Internet, but his May trial and sentencing was delayed, apparently to avoid coinciding with a US Congressional vote on granting Permanent Normal Trading Relations (PNTR) with China. He was sentenced hours after Congress had granted China PNTR status. **Guo Qinghai**, a friend and colleague of Qi, was arrested in the week before Qi's sentence on charges of 'subverting state power'. Guo's work has appeared in overseas publications. (Agence France-Presse, Associated Press, RSF, ICHRDMC)

Father Gao Yihua, a priest in China's underground Catholic church in Fujian Province, was arrested on 19 August having celebrated Mass in a friend's home. Fr Gao was reported released two days later, but his whereabouts are still unknown. **Fr Liu Saozhang** was arrested on 30 August in Fujian Province on unknown charges along with 20 nuns, two laypersons and a seminarian. Liu was reportedly severely beaten in custody. All have since been released. News emerged on 4 September that a recently ordained auxiliary bishop loyal to Rome, **Monsignor Jiang Mingyuan**, was arrested in Hebei Province on 26 August. His whereabouts are also unknown. The government reacted angrily to a report by the US State Department released on 5 September, claiming religious freedoms had deteriorated

severely. The report cited alleged persecution of Tibetan Buddhists and followers of *Falun Gong* and *Zhong Gong* in particular, and mentioned growing repression of the non-official underground churches. On 14 September, 81-year-old **Bishop Zeng Jingmu** was arrested at his home in Jiangxi Province along with two priests, **Rev. Liao Haiqing** and **Rev. Deng** (full name not known). Following the 'utmost outrage' expressed by Beijing towards the Vatican for canonising 120 Chinese martyrs on 1 October – China's National Day – China's Central Liaison Office in Hong Kong warned the Roman Catholic Church there to keep celebrations of the canonisations 'low key.' In an article in Hong Kong's *Ming Pao Daily* on 4 October, which broke news of the warning, the leader of the region's Catholics, **Bishop Joseph Zen**, accused Beijing of 'meddling with Hong Kong's religious freedoms'. (Agence France-Presse, Associated Press, BBC, Cardinal Kung Foundation, Fides, Hong Kong iMail, ICHRDMC, Reuters, *South China Morning Post*)

Danny Yung, a Hong Kong artist, was ordered on 21 August to either burn or ship back to Hong Kong 2,000 large swastikas he was intending to take to Berlin as part of an exhibit at the Hong Kong-Berlin Arts Festival. Swastikas are illegal in Germany and have recently been viewed with suspicion in China where their representation of Buddha's heart is widely used by the outlawed *Falun Gong* group. (*South China Morning Post*)

One hundred and thirty members of *Fang Cheng* – one of 14 evangelical Christian churches banned as 'evil cults' last year – were detained in Henan Province during a church service on 23 August. Among those detained were three Taiwanese-born US citizens, although the US Embassy later announced their release. Eighty-five of those detained were formally charged on 4 September with 'using an evil cult to obstruct justice' and could face prison terms. In response to the activities of the three US missionaries, the State Administration Religious Affairs (SARA) issued updated regulations on 26 September further restricting foreign churches' work in China. 'Aliens without Chinese nationality' – probably including Hong Kong residents – 'must restrict preaching to 'lawfully registered sites,' said Ye Xiaowen, head of SARA. As well as making it illegal to set up religious organisations and training centres in China, all 'illegal religious items' are liable to be confiscated by customs or by local government authorities. *(Agence France-Presse, Associated Press, Cardinal Kung Foundation, ICHRDMC, South China Morning Post)*

Prominent Hong Kong business tycoon **Li Ka-shing** threatened on 24 August to slash his companies' investments in the region if the media did not 'tone down' criticisms following a political scandal which revealed he was passed confidential economic information by a high-ranking politician. A group of politicians, academics and private individuals took out an advertisement in *Apple Daily* and *Ming Pao Daily*

saying: 'We cannot accept an individual or corporation suppressing free speech with threatening attitudes.' Li released a statement the following day about the 'misunderstanding', reaffirming his commitment to Hong Kong. (Hong Kong iMail. *South China Morning Post*)

Apparently in deference to China, the **Dalai Lama** was not invited to attend the Millennium World Peace Summit of religious leaders at the UN in New York on 28–31 August. Bishop Michael Fu Tieshan, head of the state-affiliated China Patriotic Catholic Association, said the Dalai Lama was a 'splittist [whose] presence at the meeting is inconsistent with the theme of the summit'. An address by the Dalai Lama was read by a Tibetan Buddhist leader, **Drikung Chetsun Rinpoche** – the first time in four decades the Dalai Lama has been officially represented at the UN. The Chinese delegation walked out in protest. (Agence France-Presse, Associated Press, Xinhua)

The celebrated actor and ex-vice-minister of culture, **Ying Cheng**, criticised censorship of the arts in China on BBC TV's *Hard Talk* programme on 29 August. 'We must do away with the mixing up of art and propaganda [...] Personally, I'm afraid history is not a philanthropist. It will not be kind to people who distort the truth.' (BBC)

Forty of 68 anthologies by the veteran Hong Kong columnist **Lam Shan-muk** (aka Lam Hang-chi) were impounded

at a book fair in Beijing on 29 August. It is understood his views on China's relations with Taiwan were behind the decision to confiscate the volumes. Lam's Taiwanese publishers asked for an explanation from the authorities in Beijing, and said: 'They just asked us not to stir up this matter further and not to talk to reporters any more.' (Agence France-Presse)

Zhang Hongbao, founder of the *Zhong Gong* religious group targeted by the authorities in a similar fashion to *Falun Gong*, was granted 'withholding of removal' status by a court in Hawaii on 20 September (*Index* 5/2000). Prior to the hearing, Beijing repeatedly demanded his extradition to face charges of rape from three of his followers. (In 1999, **Liu Jiaguo**, head of a smaller group called Zhushen – Supreme Spirit – was executed in Hunan Province on charges of rape.) (ICHRDMC, Reuters)

New regulations covering censorship of the Internet in China were published by Xinhua on 2 October. An extension of regulations published in January (*Index* 2/2000), the ban on posting vaguely defined 'state secrets' now covers any content deemed likely to 'threaten social stability, Communist Party authority or harm ethnic unity' – a reference to the Taiwanese and Tibetan nationalist movements. The onus is placed on the Internet Service Providers (ISPs) to block any illegal or subversive content, and requires them to keep highly detailed records of their subscribers' reading habits on the Internet – details to which the police can gain instant access. (CPJ, *Daily Telegraph*, *Financial Times*)

News emerged on 27 September of two followers of a Buddhist sect sentenced to three years in prison on 18 July in the coastal city of Ningbo. **Liu Yin** and **Gan Suqin** were charged with 'organising a cult to disrupt law and order'. They are members of the Taiwan-based *Guan Yin* sect, which claims 200,000 members throughout China. (Reuters)

COLOMBIA

Media rights groups have expressed concern about the lack of progress made by the judicial investigation into the kidnapping and torture last May of journalist **Jineth Bedoya** (*Index* 4/2000). There is strong evidence linking right-wing paramilitary forces to the abduction, as well as some law-enforcement personnel. However, investigators have apparently made no serious effort so far to interview key witnesses. (CPJ)

Popular television news host **Guillermo Cortés** was rescued by soldiers on 13 August after 200 days in captivity. The 73-year-old journalist was kidnapped in January by guerrillas of the Revolutionary Armed Forces of Colombia (*Index* 2/2000). (Associated Press)

Judicial investigators from the General Attorney's Office searched the premises of RCN television station on 16 August to obtain unedited video footage of an interview broadcast in June

with a member of a paramilitary group. The station is refusing to hand over the tapes, arguing that it would violate its duty to protect its sources. (IFJ)

Carlos Restrepo, head of the daily *Tangente* in the province of Tolima, was found dead in his house on 9 September after having been shot several times. The identity of his killers and their motives are unknown. Restrepo is the sixth journalist to be murdered this year. (WAN)

A news crew from RCN TV channel and two journalists from Medellín daily *El Colombiano* were kidnapped by National Liberation Army (ELN) guerrillas in early October. RCN reporter **Andrés Gil Gómez**, cameraman **Gustavo González** and assistant cameraman **Pedro Manuel Pinto** were abducted on 5 October while covering an ELN blockade of the Medellín–Bogotá highway. They were released 13 hours later. *El Colombiano* reporter **Jaime Horacio Arango** and photographer **Jesús Abad Colorado** were kidnapped the next day while covering the same story and were freed two days later on 8 October. The ELN said the kidnappings were a protest against the media's failure to report on army human rights abuses denounced by the guerrillas. (RSF, IFJ, CPJ)

COTE D'IVOIRE

On 8 September **Joachim Beugré**, editor of the private daily *Le Jour*, and his publisher, **Diegou Bailly**, were summoned to the presidential palace in Abidjan whereupon President

Robert Guei himself interrogated the two journalists and pressed them to reveal their sources for an article about his parentage that had appeared in that day's edition of the newspaper. The article, published under Beugré's byline, pointed out that the president's surname is different from his father's surname which appears on his birth certificate. To support Beugré's argument, a copy of the birth certificate was also published. Bailly was released without charge, after President Guei explained to him that in his tribe a son does not take his father's surname. Thereupon three soldiers acting on Guei's orders drove Beugré to his Abidjan home, which was searched. The soldiers then took the journalist to an open field near Abidjan International Airport, beat him savagely and threatened harsher retribution if he continued to report 'maliciously' about the president and his junta. Beugré spent four days in hospital. (CPJ).

Information Minister Captain Henri-Cesner Sama summoned all Abidjan-based publishers and editors-in-chief to his office on 8 September and ordered them to stop covering the activities of the army and the ruling National Public Salvation Committee (CNSP). The minister claimed that negative media coverage had 'weakened the CNSP' and added that 'civilians would be the first to suffer' if the junta was destabilised as a result of a bad press. (CPJ).

Hypolite Oulai, the daily *L'Inter*'s secretary-general, two technicians and two drivers with the Olympe press group, were beaten by soldiers on the night of 8 to 9 October in Abidjan. The five were on their way home in a company vehicle with a press badge on it when they were stopped by soldiers, who told them to lie on the ground and then beat and kicked them. One of them said: 'Since you write that soldiers are delinquents, we'll show you.' The five men underwent medical tests and are on medical leave for several days. (RSF)

CUBA

On 9 August journalist **Luis Alberto River Leiva**, owner of independent news agency Libre Oriental, was involuntarily searched and forced to hand over his identity papers to two police officers as he waited for a bus in the eastern city of Santiago de Cuba. On the same day, two state security agents posing as journalists illegally entered the old Havana premises of independent agency Cuba Press and confiscated office supplies, books and magazines. (IAPA)

RSF correspondent **Martine Jacot** was detained and interrogated on 17 August at Havana airport after spending a week interviewing members of local independent news agencies and relatives of imprisoned journalists. The French journalist was held for an hour and a half, and had her video camera, two videotapes and some documents confiscated. (RSF)

On 29 August, at approximately 7am, Swedish journalists **Birger Thureson** of the *Nya Dagen*,

Peter Gotell of the daily *Sundsvals Tidning* and **Elena Soderquist** of the daily *Arvika Nyheter*, were detained by ministry of interior officials at the Havana house where they were staying. Prior to their detention, all three had interviewed journalists from independent press organisations. (RSF)

On 18 September police stopped independent journalist **Juan Carlos Garcel** in his home town of Sagua de Tanamo, took his fingerprints and warned he would be sent to prison if he continued to work as a reporter. (CubaNet)

DEMOCRATIC REPUBLIC OF CONGO

Pierre Soshthène Kambidi, permanent correspondent of the independent daily *La Phare* in Tshikapa, was arrested on 20 August, allegedly in connection with an article he wrote implicating a judge in a diamond scandal. Kambidi said that, prior to his release on 28 September, the head of the local branch of the National Information Agency, Jean-Jacques Mbayo, burst into his cell and ordered four police officers to beat him. The journalist sustained wounds to his head and collarbone during the attack. (Journaliste en Danger)

Two arrest warrants were produced on 25 August against **Mankenda Voka**, publisher of the daily *L'Observateur*, and **Pius Mubily Mukala**, of the daily *L'Avenir*, for refusal to appear in court. They had been accused of 'leading a campaign' against a minister in the current government, Nicholas Katako, in arti-

cles that appeared in their papers. (Journaliste en Danger)

Freelance cameraman **Crispin Kandolo** was killed on 5 September during an ambush in the Kahuzi Biega Park, Bukavu Province, an area known for being controlled by the opposition Congolese Rally of Democracy. Kandolo was filming a team of technicians, officials and soldiers working in the park at the request of UNESCO. According to the governor of South Kivu, Norbert Basingizi Katintima, the men were surrounded and attacked by militiamen. Ten others were reported to have died in the attack. (WAN)

Franck Ngyke, writer of a political column for the daily *La Réference Plus*, was released on 8 September after five days detention in the cells of the National Information Agency in Kinshasa. His newspaper, which reported his arrest in the 9 September edition, did not elaborate on the reasons behind it. However, reports suggest that Ngyke's appearance in an advertisement for an organisation named 'Congo Stand Up', which has called for an end to the war and the application of the Lusaka Accord, may have played a part. (Journaliste en Danger)

On 12 September journalist **Franck Baku Fuita**, of the daily *La Réference Plus*, appeared before the Peace Court of Kinshasa — formally known as Makala Central Prison — charged with 'insulting the magistracy', 'violating the press tribunal's jurisdiction' and for the fact that the journalist does not live in Kinshasa. For reasons which were not communicated, journalists were banned from the hearing. Baku was arrested for relating information about a conflict between a former dignitary of the Mobutu regime and his wife in daily *La Référence Plus*. (Journaliste en Danger)

Emile-Aime Kaakese Vinalu, publisher of the weekly *Le Carrousel*, and **Jean-Pierre Ekanga Mukuna**, of *La Tribune de la Nation*, were sentenced to two years in prison after escaping a possible death sentence, it was reported on 21 September. They had been charged with 'demoralising the army' and making 'veiled calls to opposition leaders and sympathisers to rebel against the powers that be'. Vinalu was prosecuted for articles in the 20 June edition of the paper which complained of press censorship in the country (*Index* 5/2000). Mukana was first arrested on 23 June for refusing to give Vinalu's home address. He was released on 10 July, but rearrested on 17 August and charged with high treason. A third journalist implicated in court proceedings is **Richard Nsamba Olangi** of *Le Messager*, who was arrested on 15 August for testifying on Vinalu's behalf. (CPJ)

Minister of Communications Dominique Sakombi Inongo has replaced the management of four private radio and television stations which were recently placed under state control, it was reported on 3 October. Control of content at Television Kin Maleo, Canal Kin 1, Canal Kin 2 and the public radio station RTNC will now be vested in former associates of Sakombi. A day earlier, he signed a decree lifting the broadcasting ban on three private media: Radio Elikya, owned by the Kinshasa's Catholic Archdiocese, Radio Kintuadi, owned by the Kimbaguiste church and Television Antenne A. The three companies were among ten radio and television stations banned on 14 September for non-payment of taxes and 'not respecting the schedule of conditions governing private radio and television broadcasting'. (Journaliste en Danger)

It was reported on 12 October that the daily *L'Avenir* in Kinshasa was under siege in early October by the commander of the Seventh Military Region. Among the 13 staff arrested were the director of financial administration, **Brigitte Mwabilu**, and members of the editorial team. Computers, communications equipment, passports and money were taken. All were subsequently released except computer technician **Sosthene Baniwesize**, who was detained until 3 October. (Journaliste en Danger)

EAST TIMOR

The UN announced on 15 September that it would re-investigate the killing of five Australian reporters in Balibo on 16 October 1975 in the run-up to Indonesia's full-scale invasion of the former Portuguese colony. The case of **Roger East**, a freelance Australian journalist, executed during the actual invasion on 7 December 1975, might also be opened. The five journalists went into East Timor to examine the rumours about an impending Indonesian attack. A witness saw members of the invading troops take the journalists off to a house and, after hearing shots, saw three bodies dumped outside. Another witness reported that the wounds were made with a pistol, rather than the government's excuse of machine-gun 'crossfire'. Other witnesses have said that the troops went to Balibo specifically to eliminate the journalists. (*Melbourne Age*, CPJ, Reuters)

EGYPT

Attempts by the Labour Party to republish *Al Shahab*, the party's newspaper, were thwarted in early August when *Al-Ahram*, the government-owned printing house, refused to print the journal. The newspaper was closed down in May by the Political Parties Commission (*Index* 4/2000), but a High Court ruling on 25 July declared the action unconstitutional, allowing publication to recommence. However, the intervention of the printers, who announced that they would not produce the paper until its legal status became 'clear', meant that *Al Shahab* did not return to the newsstands as planned. (*Cairo Times*)

On 8 August the Administrative Court overturned a ban imposed on opposition weekly *Sawt Al Umma* in February 1999. The Higher Press Council withdrew the newspaper's licence in 1999 after it was taken over by **Essam Fahmi**, an ardent critic of the government (*Index* 3/1999). The Administrative Court ordered the council to reinstate *Sawt Al Umma*'s credentials immediately. (*Cairo Times*)

Saad Ed Din Ibrahim, who was arrested in June and accused of 'spying for the USA' and 'distributing propaganda' (*Index* 5/2000), was released on 10 August. Ibrahim, head of the Ibn Khaldun Centre, a non-governmental organisation promoting democracy, was held in police custody for six weeks. All formal charges against him and his four associates were dropped, but officials have not ruled out the possibility of launching further investigations. (Digital Freedom Network, Egyptian Organisation for Human Rights)

The family of Gamil Al Batouty, co-pilot of EgyptAir flight 990 which crashed in October 1999, announced on 15 August that it is suing US magazine *Newsweek* and CNN for 'defamation of character'. Drawing on evidence from the official investigation into the accident, both the magazine and the news channel reported that Al Batouty had deliberately caused the aircraft to plunge into the Atlantic. (*Cairo Times*)

Magdi Hussein, the jailed managing editor of *Al Shahab*, announced on 25 September that he intended to run for a seat in parliament from behind bars. Hussein was sentenced along with two other *Al Shahab* colleagues to two years' imprisonment for 'slandering' Agriculture Minister Yussef Wali in August 1999 (*Index* 4/1999, 5/1999). (*Cairo Times*)

EQUATORIAL GUINEA

About half of the 1,200 copies of *Truth* magazine were seized and retained in police stations in the town of Bata. No reason was given for the seizure of edition no. 40, published around 1 August, but it mentioned internal fights between members of the ruling party, the PDGE, electoral fraud and the scandalous purchase by the son of President Teodorin Obiang of a US$20m apartment on Fifth Avenue, New York. (*Index*/Spain)

ETHIOPIA

Two leading Amharic newspapers, *Reporter* and *Tobia*, warned on 22 August that the high cost of producing papers would force the private press to fold. The weekly *Reporter* said that 'the newsprint and printing costs are detrimental to the freedom of the press in Ethiopia'. The parastatal Baerhamene Selam Press, which prints nearly all the country's newspapers, had informed clients of a new price hike on 16 August. (PANA)

GEORGIA

On 16 August **Sozar Subeliani**, a reporter with RFE/RL, was beaten by about 40 members of the radical orthodox group, Eparchy of Gldani, led by defrocked priest Basili Mkaveishvili, better known as 'Father Basili'. He was covering the trial of followers of Father Basili who are accused of assaulting Jehovah's Witnesses in Tblisi last autumn. The next day, **David Paichadze**, another RFE/RL reporter covering the proceedings, was beaten by the same mob. They also set upon two human rights activists from the Liberty Institute. (RFE/RL, HRW)

Journalists of the independent newspaper *Resonansi* were forced onto the street on 25 September when a group, led by defrocked priest Father Basili, burst into the editorial office. They were reportedly angry at an article by **Ghia Lakobashvili** condemning their repeated assaults on Jehovah's Witnesses. (CIPDD)

Vasily Silgadze, a reporter with independent daily *Eko Digest*, has been fired. He believes his dismissal is connected to an investigation into a recent incident when he was beaten by men angered by his article on police corruption (*Index* 5/2000). (CJES)

GERMANY

A British photojournalist was attacked by neo-Nazi sympathisers as he tried to gather pictures of far-right extremists for news agencies. Freelancer **Justin Jim** became involved in a brawl on 28 August in the Brandenburg village of Rathenow. He was with three African asylum seekers when confronted by a gang of youths. Jim was hit in the face before local police intervened. An east German youth was subsequently arrested for the affray. (*Guardian*)

Three new guidebooks to Germany, *Lonely Planet*, *Let's Go Germany* and *Explorer Germany*, have offended politicians by warning of the potential threat to ethnic minority and homosexual people visiting the country. According to the *Let's Go Germany* guidebook, 'in certain economically depressed regions, tourists of colour or members of certain religious groups may feel threatened'. Willi Polte, the mayor of Magdeburg, one of the cities singled out by the *Lonely Planet* guide, condemned the idea of the possibility of attacks as 'absurd'. (*Daily Telegraph*)

GHANA

On 24 September four armed soldiers led by Deputy Minister of Defence Dr Tony Aidoo stormed the offices of the *Crusading Guide* and bundled news editor **Sedi Bansah** into a car. He was driven around town and finally deposited at police headquarters, where he was told to report back the next morning. The arrest came hours after he phoned Dr Aidoo in a bid to cross-check a story he was writing about an alleged attack by the deputy minister on a civilian security guard at the Dansoman Goil petrol station. (*Ghanaian Chronicle*)

During the early hours of 2 October, unidentified persons smeared human excrement on the entrance of the offices of the Accra bi-weekly *Crusading Guide*. The incident is the third time under the present government that human waste has been used as weapon of intimidation against the private press. Other media houses to have suffered the same fate – known in the local press as 'shit bombing' – are the *Ghanaian Chronicle* and the *Free Press*. (*West African Journalists Association*)

GREECE

Slavko Mangovski, editor-in-chief of the Macedonian weekly magazine *Makedonsko Sonce*, was refused entry into Greece at the Evzoni border crossing on 25 August. He was intending to visit a village festival in northern Greece, but was forced to wait while border authorities checked his details with Central Police in Athens. Mangovski decided to return home rather than continue waiting. Three days later he tried to cross at the Niki border crossing, intent on visiting another village festival. Mangovski was given a Notification Certificate for the Refusal of Entry which specified 'other reasons' as the grounds for his refusal. A crossed stamp was placed in his US passport so as to alert border authorities in future of his ban from entering Greece. (GHM)

A public concert planned by the Citizens' Movement, European Expression and the Serbian student opposition movement Otpor was refused a licence by the Prefect of Salonica, Costas Papadopoulos. The concert was initially planned to take place in the port area of the city, but pro-communist groups threatened to disrupt it with counter-demonstrations. The organisers then tried to get permission for it to be held in the state-owned Lazarists' Monastery on 16 September, but Papadopoulos also refused permission, stating that the concert would be 'an intrusion in the internal affairs of another country'. (GHM)

INDIA

On 20 August **Thounaojam Brajamani Singh**, editor of the English-language daily *Manipur News* and president of the Manipur State Journalists' Association, was killed in Imphal. He was followed on his motorbike by two men, who then forced him to stop before shooting him twice in the back of the head at point-blank range. Brajamani Singh had received anonymous death threats on 15 August and, the day before his murder, the editor had published an article urging those who made the threats to desist. The motive for the murder of the man known as the 'pioneer of English journalism in Manipur' is unknown. (CPJ, RSF)

Daily newspaper *Malaya Manorama* was effectively banned from the campus of the University of Calicut when an order was issued cancelling the university's subscription, it was reported on 11 October. The university press officer was directed to refrain from sending press releases to the newspaper's offices. A copy of the order was sent to the security officer, and it is believed that distribution of the paper on campus will be prevented. (IPI)

INDONESIA

Radio journalist **Max Arthur** was attacked in Kupang by a pro-Jakarta militia on 30 August. He had been called a spy by East Timor refugees and supporters of integration while attending a protest outside the provincial parliament office. A mob attacked him, taking some of his equipment. The protest had been in defiance of East Timor's Independence Day and of former president BJ Habibie, who had permitted the UN to hold the new country's independence referendum more than a year ago. Arthur suffered damage to his face, jaw, arms and ribs. (Southeast Asian Press Alliance)

On 28 September **Ferry Indrawang** of online paper Bisik.com, and **Andi Lala** of Jakarta News FM, were beaten by police officers while covering an anti-Suharto student rally outside the Agricultural Department Building in Ragunan, South Jakarta. The violence escalated as police officers began attacking protesters and journalists, and spraying tear gas. Indrawang was kicked in the back and, upon announcing that he was a journalist, was pounced on by about ten officers and punched and beaten with bats. When he was loaded onto a Red Cross ambulance, an officer hit him over the head. Andi Lala was dragged out of a telephone café where he and other journalists were hiding to keep out of the rain and away from the brutality. He was beaten by officers despite showing his press card. He suffered bruises to the face and lost two teeth. Indrawang was unconscious most of the day, had six stitches in his head and suffered concussion. (Alliance of Independent Journalists)

IRAN

On 8 August the press court banned the reformist daily *Bahar* for allegedly fabricating an interview with parliamentary deputy

Ahmad Pournejati. He was quoted as saying that reformists were determined to bring a new press bill in defiance of Ayatollah Khamenei's order. (*International Herald Tribune*)

On 9 August veteran secular journalist **Masoud Behnoud** (*Index* 5/2000) was imprisoned by the Press Court, having had 85 charges filed against him. The Iranian press agency, IRNA, gave no further details. (Reuters)

The pro-reformist weekly *Ava* was closed on 17 August by a hardline court, and its publisher, **Mostafa Izadi**, was barred from press activities. (Reuters)

On 23 August it was reported that the former editor-in-chief of the now banned reformist newspaper *Neshat*, **Mashallah Shamsolvaezin**, has been placed in solitary confinement. Shamsolvaezin was jailed in April for 'hurting Islam'. (WAN)

Hadi Khamenei, publisher of the moderate daily *Hayat-e No* and brother of Ayatollah Ali Khamenei, was summonsed before the Special Court of the Clergy on 11 September to face vague charges of 'press offences'. (MERIP)

Embattled reformists launched a new paper on 4 October in an attempt to replace three of their papers closed in the last 16 months. **Hamid-Reza Jaleipour** (*Index* 5/1998, 4/2000), financial backer, editor and columnist, used a licence they had bought as a precaution two years ago, and has named the new publication *Asr-e*

Azadegan. (*International Herald Tribune*)

IRELAND

Thirty-three years after it was made, the film version of James Joyce's *Ulysses* has been passed by the censors. The film was banned in 1967 and the Censorship Appeals Board refused it a certificate in the same year. A further submission for a certificate made in 1975 was refused, and an appeal in 1977 was not granted. Chief censor Sheamus Smith commented that, if the film had been resubmitted at any time in the last 14 years, he would have lifted the ban. (BBC)

ISRAEL

Israeli soldiers on 12 September shot into the air over the heads of three Lebanese journalists apparently to discourage them from taking pictures in an undisclosed location on the frontier. On 22 September, soldiers shot at the legs of Lebanese journalists without any warning. (RSF)

JORDAN

The Senate endorsed a bill on 20 August to license private television and radio stations, four days after the Chamber of Deputies approved the bill. The 17-article law also vaguely refers to apparent limitations on media coverage, saying the private stations can only broadcast material that 'serves the Kingdom's media goals'. (Associated Press)

On 5 September the Jordan Press Association (JPA) expelled its secretary-general, **Nidal**

• •

SEYYED EBRAHIM NABAVI
Personal problem

Q.   When did you first sense that you had a personal problem with [former president Akbar Hashemi-Rafsanjani]?

A.   It was in 1979 that I developed a personal problem with him.

Q.   How did your personal problem with him come about?

A.   He gave an order for everyone who was 20 years old to be turned upside down and thrown in a well. There were about 1,213,473 of us and we developed a personal problem with him.

Q.   Was your personal problem resolved later?

A.   Yes, when I came out of the well, I went to an office to get a job. I was there for a year. But since me and 8,342 other people were giving them dirty looks, they sacked us and that was when we developed personal problems again.

Q.   Did you also have personal problems with him after this period?

A.   Yes. I'd written a book and I wanted to have it published. I went to his ministry. He told me and the other 6,647 people who were there that we weren't allowed to publish our books and I developed personal problems again.

Q.   What other personal problems did you have?

A.   After giving up on the book, we started a magazine, which was banned because of personal problems.

Q.   How many of you were there?

A.   17,742,611

Q.   Did you also have very personal problems with him?

A.   Yes, since he saw that I was really impudent, he ordered me put into jail. I said: 'Excuse me, but the way to deal with impudent people is to beat them up, not to throw them in jail.' He said: 'Don't worry, you'll be beaten there as well, as sure as night follows day.' When I went to jail, I saw that there were about 43,000 people there who all had personal problems.

Q.   How many people do you think have personal problems with him?

A.   About 28 to 38 million. ❑

This is an edited version of an article by Iranian satirist **Sayeed Ebrahim Nabavi** *(Index 5/2000, which appeared on 5 February in* Asr-e Azadegan, *one of 17 liberal journals closed down between 20 April and 9 May (Index 4/2000). On 12 August, Nabavi was arrested after interrogation by the Press Court. Translated by Nilou Mobasser*

• •

Mansour (*Index* 5/2000), effectively banning him from the profession for life as all journalists are legally required to be JPA members. Mansour, who is also chief editor of the weekly *Al-Hadath*, was dismissed for accepting funds from overseas to launch his Centre for Defending Freedom of Journalists, and for not being a full-time journalist. (IPI, A19)

KAZAKHSTAN

Since 15 September, access to the website www.eurasia.org has been blocked. Access is through two communication lines Kazakhtelecom and Nursat owned by joint-stock companies and under state control. (CJES, Internews)

On the evening of 15 September **Lira Baiseitova**, editor-in-chief of independent newspaper *Respublika* 2000, was attacked and threatened with death. The incident occurred following publication of an article she had written implicating Nurla Kaparov, director of a regional refinery. The article suggested that a road accident in which a passenger in Kaparov's car died had resulted from Kaparov's drunk driving. (RSF, CJES)

On 18 August independent daily *Do i Posle Ponedel 'nika* was banned from publishing articles which 'inflict hurt' on the state. Earlier this year, the paper faced similar charges and had to change its name from *Nachiom s Ponedel 'nika* (*Index* 4/2000). Editor-in-chief **Ramazan Esergepov** will appeal to Almaty City Court. (CJES)

KENYA

Hundreds of demonstrators marched through the streets of Nairobi in late August in protest at the killing of **Father John Kaiser**, a US Roman Catholic bishop and leading human rights critic of President Moi's government. Father Kaiser was found shot dead in Naivasha, 50 miles from Nairobi. Independent newspapers reported that the bishop was carrying documents at the time of his death linking two unidentified ministers to a plot to pay tribal warriors to carry out ethnic cleansing in Rift Valley Province. (*The Times*)

On 31 August President Moi accused private stations broadcasting in languages other than English and Kiswahili of undermining national unity and encouraging tribal chauvinism. As a consequence, he announced new legislation which would effectively ban private vernacular broadcasting. The commentary, made at the opening of the Agricultural Society of Kenya Show in Mombasa, is thought to be an open attack on the highly popular radio station Kameme FM, which broadcasts in Kikuyu, Kenya's most widely spoken vernacular language. (CPJ)

The weekly *Independent*, published by the Immediate Media Services, has been barred from publishing articles considered defamatory about Bishop Arthur Kitonga of the Redeemed Gospel Church. The newspaper was accused of a campaign of harassment against the bishop despite a suit filed by the court last week. Kitonga said that the newspaper has implied

that he is a criminal and that he was initiated into the church for the sole purpose of making money. (NDIMA)

Managing director of Radio Kameme FM **Rose Kimotho** told a press conference that the station has instituted legal action for defamation against a monthly newspaper, *Expression Today*, published by the Media Institute. She is hoping to sue the paper over two articles in the September issue under the headlines 'The intrigue behind radio ban,' and 'Succession politics behind vernacuar radio ban'. (NDIMA)

KIRIBATI

Michael Field, a journalist from New Zealand, had his ban from the South Pacific Forum meeting on the island in October reaffirmed, it was reported on 8 October. The media co-ordinator in the presidential office, Tikiau Takeke, said Field was banned because he was 'responsible for writing unfair, untrue and derogatory' stories about Kiribati and its people. Field visited Kiribati last year and wrote about the extensive pollution, sewage and litter on the main island of Tarawa, where the forum will be held. (Pacific Media Watch)

KYRGYSTAN

Authorities ruled that from the 12 August all news on clashes with insurgents would be distributed through President Askar Akaev's press service. (CJES)

On 19 September officers from the ministry of national security (MNS) searched the offices of popular independent weekly, *Delo No.* They were looking for documents relating to articles written by **Vadim Nochevkin**, which claimed that a secret agent from the MNS was connected with a report on unregistered bugging equipment obtained in Moscow. Security officials also searched the apartments of Nochevkin and chief editor **Viktor Zapolsky**. (RFE/RL, CJES)

LIBERIA

On 18 August a four-member news crew from Britain's Channel Four were arrested by police at their hotel and charged with espionage, a first-degree felony with a minimum ten-year sentence. The crew included award-winning Sierra Leonean journalist **Gugulakhe Radebesa**, **Sorious Samora**, a South African, and **David Barrie** and **Tim Lambon** who are both British. Equipment and videotapes were also seized and Justice Minister Eddington Varmeh held a press conference in which he described the videotapes as 'damaging' to the government and the security of the state. Sources say the journalists had initially written to the government expressing interest in probing allegations of diamond smuggling and gun-running between the government and rebels in Sierra Leone. The journalists possessed valid visas and had written permission to film a documentary. The crew was released after having 'apologised', according to Liberian President

Charles Taylor in a television interview. (Associated Press, CPJ, PANA)

MAURITANIA

The authorities have invoked Article 11 of the press law to seize issue 137 of the private weekly *La Tribune.* According to editor **Mohammed F Ould**, the seizure was in reaction to an editorial which gave a critical assessment of the government's achievements since coming to power in 1978. (RSF)

MALAWI

Lamp and *Together* journalist **Prince Jamali** was arrested on 14 September, along with three other journalists, on charges of theft. Jamali claims that the charges are false and that he is being persecuted for writing a story on police brutality. (MISA)

Rankin Nyekanyek, editor of the *Daily Times*, has been severely demoted following his suspension over an editorial decision in August. Nyekanyek was suspended for not leading with a story about President Bakili Muluzi opening a local plastic factory. Instead Nyekanyek led with a story about Malawi police due to serve in Kosovo. (MISA)

MEXICO

At around 7pm on 19 September State Judicial police arrested **Jesús Antonio Pinedo Cornejo**, editor of the weekly Cuidad Juárez newspaper *Seminario*, in connection with an article by *Seminario* journalist **Luis Villagrana**, which linked former

police chief Javier Benavides González with the drugs trade. Benavides had taken out a case for criminal defamation against the two. Pinedo was held overnight and released after posting a bond of US$1,600. Villagrana appeared voluntarily before the court and also posted bail. On 3 October, the police chief dropped the charges. (CPJ)

MOROCCO

Aboubakr Jamal, director of the weekly *Le Journal*, was publicly threatened on 4 October by Interior Minister Ahmed Midaoui during a press conference at which the latter was being questioned about the government's stance on the Polisario Front, which seeks independence for Western Sahara. Earlier in the year, *Le Journal* incensed the government by carrying an interview with the leader of the Front, a move that earned the publication a temporary ban (*Index* 4/2000, 5/2000). On this occasion, Midaoui threatened to shut the paper down for good if another article sympathetic to the organisation appeared, as well as warning Jamal that he'd 'smash his face in' for good measure. (RSF)

On 8 October three French journalists were placed under house arrest on orders of the public prosecutor for the country's eastern provinces. **Joseph Thual**, **Jean-Marc Pitt** and **Michel Bernasconi**, all of whom work for the television station France 3, were reporting on a pilgrimage organised by the Truth and Justice Forum to the Tazmamart Prison, a penitentiary notorious for the brutality of its conditions. No explanation was offered for the action. This year, Thual has suffered persistent harassment from the Moroccan authorities: in June, customs officials seized video cassettes from him and subjected him to a number of unnecessary searches (*Index* 5/2000). (RSF)

On 11 October the authorities prevented **Iqbal Ilhami**, correspondent for the Qatari television station Al-Jazeera, from broadcasting her report. Citing 'technical difficulties', the state television station whose studios Ilhami uses to record her reports refused to transmit her weekly dispatch. She was subsequently told by the interior ministry that she was banned from journalism until further notice. (Middle East Intelligence Wire)

NAMIBIA

On 27 September the Namibian Labour Court ordered the Namibian Broadcasting Corporation to reinstate senior staff member **Norah Appolus** to the post of news chief at the public broadcaster. Appolus was removed from the post in October for what she claims were political reasons. (MISA)

NETHERLANDS

Journalist **Koen Voskuil** was released on 9 October after media organisations and journalists united in pressing the government for his release. He was detained on 22 September by the Amsterdam Court of Justice for refusing to reveal his sources for two articles published in *Spits*

about a criminal investigation. Voskuil must, however, still appear in a criminal court case to give a testimony. (IFJ)

PAKISTAN

A 'routine' electrical inspection by an army inspection team sent to the headquarters of the Dawn Group of Newspapers in Karachi on 27 September appears to have been used as a means of harassing and intimidating staff. Six armed personnel accompanied the inspector and engineers. They threatened to cut off the power supply to the building if they were not granted access to all areas immediately. Photographers were forbidden from capturing the inspection on camera by the military officer in charge. The newspaper group includes the English-language daily *Dawn*, which had published an article on 12 September entitled 'Free press: Is Musharraf having second thoughts?', which apparently angered administration officials. On 19 September *Dawn* received a letter from the minister of information claiming that the article defamed officials in the information ministry and threatening legal action if they did not publish a clarification. (CPJ, PPF, WAN, WEF)

Correspondent for *Aaj* and *Din* daily newspapers **Shujaat Ali Khan** was arrested on 29 August in Bisham and accused of 'impersonation' following a judge's order which concerned a paper for which he does not work. It is thought that his arrest is linked to the publication of an appeal by a widow to General Musharraf to help him arrest her son's and

husband's killers. The judge in charge of the widow's case also ordered the journalist's arrest. Shujaat Ali Khan is now in the Central Jail in Saidu Sharif. (RSF)

PALESTINE

At least ten journalists were wounded in late September/early October's violent clashes between Palestinians, initially protesting against the state-sanctioned visit by the extremist Likud leader Ariel Sharon to the Haram al-Sharif holy site, and Israeli soldiers. On 29 September five journalists were injured by security forces while covering disturbances around the Al-Aqsa mosque in Jerusalem. **Hazem Bader**, an Associated Press cameraman, was shot at close range in his right hand by a sniper's rubber-coated metal bullet. **Khaled Abu Aker**, a correspondent with the TV station France 2, was beaten by police after refusing to hand over a rubber-coated bullet he had picked up off the ground. Associated Press journalist **Khaled al-Zeghary** was shot in his right leg by a rubber-coated metal bullet, and then beaten by six policemen who removed his camera. Photographer **Mahfouz Abu-Turk** was shot in his leg by two rubber-coated bullets from about 30 meteres by special forces, and an Agence France-Presse photographer, **Awad Awad**, was shot by rubber-coated bullets in his right leg and right arm from close range. On 1 October ABC News cameraman **Amer al-Ja'bari** was wounded in the head at the Hebron bypass road while standing at least 400 metres from clashes. He left hospital the following day after surgery. On 2 October **Mazen Dana**, a Reuters cameraman, was hit in the left foot and leg by live ammunition fired by Israeli forces – having been shot in the same leg only the day before. He believes the attacks may have been deliberate. Also on 2 October, **Loay Abu Haykel**, a Reuters photojournalist, was hit in the leg by a rubber-coated bullet while covering the clashes. The same day in Hebron, **Wa'el al-Shiokhy**, journalist with the local station TV al-Nawras, was also shot. (RSF, CPJ)

PANAMA

On 8 August police surrounded the home of **Gustavo Gorriti**, associate editor of Panama City's daily *La Prensa*, and those of two of his colleagues, reporters **Rolando Rodríguez** and **Mónica Palm**, in a bid to compel them to testify in a criminal-defamation suit by Attorney General José Antonio Sossa. The suit is based on *La Prensa*'s 1999 coverage of Sossa's alleged links to two convicted US drug traffickers. *La Prensa*'s business editor, **Miren Guttiérrez**, is also a defendant in the case, but the police were unable to locate her home. The police officers had a summons order issued on 1 August by prosecutor Armando Fuentes, which was executed despite the habeas corpus writ filed the previous day by the journalists' lawyer, Alejandro Watson. In accordance with the structure of the Panamanian judicial system, Attorney Fuentes is subordinate to Attorney General Sossa, who filed the suit against the journalists. (RSF,CPJ)

It was reported on 2 October that **Mariella Patriau Hildebrandt**, editor of Lima daily *Liberación*, and photojournalist **Adriana Navarro de Vivanco**, were assaulted in Panama City by the lawyer of Vladimiro Montesinos, a former advisor for President Alberto Fujimori and de facto head of Peru's secret services. The lawyer, Jaime Aleman, warned them to leave his office, even though they had previously arranged an appointment. Six individuals immediately confiscated Navarro's camera as she attempted to take a photograph of Aleman. The camera was later returned to them broken, and without the film. (IFJ)

PARAGUAY

A series of attacks and threats against several media followed the closely fought vice-presidential election on 13 August, in which the candidate of the ruling Colorado Party was narrowly defeated by his opposition rival. On election day, a 'rogue' signal interfered with the frequency of Asunción-based Radio Primero de Marzo as it was preparing to broadcast the results of an exit poll after the close of voting. Anonymous voices carried by the signal threatened to blow up the station's transmitting equipment and 'disappear' its news host. On 15 August Colorado Party supporters, angry at the electoral result, threw stones and bottles at the offices of Radio Nandutí, also in Asunción. The station was one of only a few local media that predicted the victory of Liberal Party candidate, Julio César Franco. Also, the daily

Noticias de Asunción received several bomb threats on 18 and 20 August, and one of its reporters, **Marlene Franco**, had her house shot at fives times on 19 August. (SPP, CPJ)

Elizabeth Palma, a reporter with Canal 9 television station, suffered a broken hip and spinal injuries after being run over on 17 August by the security chief of then Comptroller General Daniel Fretes. It is thought that bodyguard Calixto Arguello deliberately rammed his vehicle into Palma to discourage her and other journalists from questioning Fretes, who faces trial on 19 separate counts of corruption. Palma is expected to be bedridden for a month. (CPJ, SPP)

Daily *ABC Color* editor **Aldo Zuccolillo** was banned on 28 August from leaving the country and fined nearly US$3,000 for allegedly violating electoral law with the publication of two opinion pieces prior to the 13 August vice-presidential election. The judge in charge also ordered Zuccolillo to return to court on the 28th of each month. The editor was accused of breaking the law prohibiting the publication of 'electoral propaganda' 48 hours before an election by running two editorials on 12 and 13 August supporting opposition candidate Julio César Franco. (RSF)

Journalist **Camilo Cantero**, who heads Radio Libertad and writes for the daily *Ultima Hora* in San Ignacio, was banned on 31 August from speaking or writing in the media about a libel case he is currently facing. The judge in charge of the case imposed the prohibition in exchange for releasing Cantero from prison, where he spent six days after being charged on 25 August. The journalist is being sued by Judge Mario Ignacio Maidana, whom Cantero accused last year of failing to perform his duties adequately. (SPP)

PERU

Cecilia Valenzuela, editor of online news agency imedia-peru.com, has allegedly been under surveillance since running a series of articles on the role of National Intelligence Service (SIN) in an arms and drug trafficking case. Since 31 August a van with tinted windows has been parked in front of the agency's offices and, on 4 September, a vehicle allegedly tried to run Valenzuela over in front of her house. (RSF)

A television crew from local TV channel Canal Fénix was physically attacked and had video equipment seized by police on 4 September after filming a raid to evict squatters from a property in the town of Majes. A contingent of police officers, accompanied by about 20 hooded men wielding sticks and branches, stormed the property, shooting into the air and firing teargas canisters. When they realised they were being filmed, a number of officers grabbed filming and recording equipment from cameraman **Esmeregildo Paz Pinto** and his assistant **Alejandro Anconeyra Provincia**, and began manhandling reporter **Vicky Bazán Cossi**, who is also an editor with Majes-based

Radio Rimelsa and a correspondent for the daily *La República*. (IFJ)

Two journalists from daily *El Popular* were allegedly beaten, kidnapped and robbed on 12 September by the mayor of the Lima district of San Juan de Lurigancho and two of his bodyguards. Editor **Alexis Fiestas Quinto** and photographer **Víctor Granda** were attacked while interviewing local residents who were demonstrating against Mayor Ricardo Chiroque's decision to demolish some public washrooms. Chiroque and his henchmen allegedly stormed out of the town hall and grabbed and kicked the two journalists, dragging them indoors, where they were held against their will for two hours. The mayor allegedly threatened to kill them with a revolver, which he then reportedly wrapped in cloth to use as a bludgeon. The journalists were robbed of a camera, notebook, press badges and jewellery. Chiroque has denied the charges. (IPYS, IFJ)

The loudspeaker system used by local radio programme *Hora Siete* in the Amazonian district of Requena was seized by authorities on 13 September. The local state attorney accused the programme's host, journalist **Luis Gastelú Rodríguez**, of operating the loudspeakers without a proper licence. However, Gastelú says the seizure is an attempt to silence the only medium in the area that dares speak out against the local ruling party-controlled municipality. The journalist claims to have been continually harassed by

mayor Juan Amasifuen Laulate and severely beaten on 11 September by four individuals who reportedly work for the municipality. (IPYS)

Gente magazine withdrew a libel action on 20 September against current affairs television programme *Vértice*, broadcast by Canal N, after it emerged that a high-ranking magistrate had tried to turn the case into a witch-hunt. The magazine sued for defamation and damages after a guest on the programme accused *Gente* of acting as a mouthpiece of the SIN. The defendants were *Vértice*'s producer, **Hugo Guerra**, Canal N's general manager, **Alberto Cendra**, and the programme's guest, **Gustavo Gorriti**, former press advisor to opposition party Perú Posible and associate editor of Panama City's daily *La Prensa*. However, the case was discredited by magistrate Alejandro Rodríguez Medrano's alleged attempt to use it as a platform for a summary investigation against the accused. This came to light after the judge in charge of the case, Sonia Medina Calvo, was dismissed for refusing to go along with Rodríguez's plan. The magistrate is widely believed to have close links with former presidential advisor and SIN intimate Vladimiro Montesinos. (IPYS)

Daily *La República* editor **Rosa Reyna** was verbally and physically attacked by ruling party congressman Luis Cáceres Velásquez on 22 September. The incident took place in the corridors of congress after a Reyna approached the politician for an interview together with other journalists. Cáceres started hurling insults at Reyna and *La República* and dragged the journalist into his office, where he held her against her will. Reyna had to later be treated for an anxiety attack. Ten days later, the congressman publicly apologised for the incident. (IPYS)

Independent television station Red Global, which broadcasts the Canal 13 channel, was declared bankrupt on 25 September and placed under the control of a board of creditors dominated by government sympathisers. The station's former chief and majority shareholder, businessman **Genaro Delgado Parker**, accused the National Intelligence Service of orchestrating the bankruptcy action to turn Canal 13 into a government mouthpiece. Red Global was declared insolvent by the consumer watchdog, INDECOPI. INDECOPI had earlier dismissed the bankruptcy case as fraudulent, but was forced to go ahead with it under orders from Lima's First Civil Corporate Court. (IPYS)

PHILIPPINES

Jean-Jacques Le Garrec and **Roland Madura**, two French journalists kidnapped on the island of Jolo, managed to escape on 19 September while their captors were distracted by a military strike. After hiding for ten hours in the forest, they were picked up by government trucks and flown to Manila. They had been captured on 9 July with colleague **Maryse Burgot** while trying to interview hostages of the Abu Sayyaf, fighting for an independent Islamic state. Burgot and four hostages were freed on 27 August after their ransoms had been paid by Libya. (Pacific Media Watch)

Professor Safwan Idris, rector of the Ar Raniry State Institute of Islamic Studies, was assassinated on 16 September in the Aceh region. His murderers may have been connected with the Brimob (Mobile Brigade), police forces from Banda Aceh. While a leading candidate for governor in Aceh, Idris was also a member of the Independent Investigative Commission, which worked to examine human rights violations and military atrocities in the area. (Pacific Media Watch)

POLAND

The use of the words 'supermarket', 'music club' and 'plaza' have been effectively outlawed after a language-purity law came into force in August. 'Language police' from the newly formed 'Language Council' will monitor progress. Those found violating the law could face heavy fines. At the same time a broadcasting law was passed which states that one-third of music played on radio stations must be Polish. (*Guardian*)

RUSSIA

The grieving mother of a sailor, who perished with all hands on the nuclear submarine Kursk near Murmansk, was silenced on 19 August by being forcibly injected with a sedative while begging Deputy Prime Minister Ilya Klebanov: 'How long are we going to have to endure this?' Russian television captured the approach of a medic from behind who then injected her: she immediately fell to the floor. (*Guardian*)

In a related incident, President Vladimir Putin threatened to punish **Grigori Nekhoroshev** of daily *Nezavisimaya Gazeta* and **Andrei Kolesnikov** of *Kommersant* who, posing as relatives of the dead, saw his emotional encounter with 500 relatives of the dead when no outsiders were allowed near Vidyayevo. He claimed they were 'unscrupulously trying to exploit this misfortune ... to gain political capital'. (*Guardian*)

Masked commandos, carrying automatic weapons charged into the office of the human rights organisation Glasnost Defense Foundation on 28 August while they were discussing plans for an emergency congress of human rights activists. A dozen people, including a ten-year-old child, were held face down on the floor for approximately 40 minutes. The men searched the documents of **Ernst Cjyorny**, leader of Ecology and Human Rights, who was present during the raid. They left when asked to show identification. (CCSI)

ORT journalists **Vadim Chelikov** and **Vladimir Agafono** were denied accreditation to work in Chechnya, and it was announced on 31 August that General Manilov, head of the unified Russian military command in Chechnya, would take personal responsibility for the decision. The reason given was 'unauthorised filming on the territory of the Khankali military base' where the reporters filmed burning train cars doused with gasoline. (CJES)

Ruslan Musayev, a local reporter and cameraman for Associated Press, was captured by Russian military forces in Chechnya on 5 September while travelling to Grozny from south Chechnya to cover anticipated military operations. He was beaten and held in detention overnight at military headquarters in Khankali, but released the following morning after interrogation by an officer who took his watch and US$600. He was then driven to the Ingushetia border where he was released. Officials in Chechnya and Moscow later denied the arrest had taken place. (CPJ, WPFC, RFE/RL)

The government announced on 6 September that special subsidies to the media will be included in the 2001 federal budget, but they will be classified as top secret, a classification usually reserved for defence expenditure. (RFE/RL)

A high-ranking government official gave Boris Berezovsky an ultimatum: to hand over his block of Russian Public Television (ORT) shares to the state or 'go the same way as **Vladimir Gusinsky**' (*Index* 4/2000, 5/2000). On 7 September Berezovsky named more than 20 people to whom he will transfer 49% of his ORT shares. Among those named are: *Kommersant* journalist **Natalya Gevorkian**, *Novyeizvestiya* editor **Igor Golembiovskii**, *Nexavisimaya gazeta* editor **Vitalii Tretyakov**, ORT journalist **Sergei**

Dorenko, former ORT general director and former deputy head of presidential administration **Igor Shabdurasulov**, novelists **Vasilii Asenov**, **Facil Iskander**, **Viktor Pelevin** and film director **Rustam Khamdamov**, as well as other representatives of the creative intelligentsia. The Kremlin stated that it accepted Berezovsky's intention, but President Putin stressed that the nominees must be independent: several are editors of publications controlled by Berezovsky or employees of Vladimir Gusinsky's Media-MOST group. (RFE/RL)

In a related move, Vladimir Gusinsky was forced to sign over his Media-MOST group in return for his release from jail and the lifting of his travel ban. The Kremlin-controlled gas giant, Gazprom, has since taken control of the media empire. A company spokesman claimed that the US$290m deal was made on 20 July but that Gusinsky has said he will refuse to fulfil it. (*Guardian*)

Journalist **Iskandr Khatloni** was attacked on 21 September by an assailant with an axe in his Moscow apartment and died later that night in Botkin Hospital. Khatloni, who had worked for Radio Free Europe/Radio Liberty for the Tajik service since 1996, was investigating stories about military human rights abuses in Chechnya. (CJES)

According to an undated survey by the Public Opinion Foundation, only 1% of the population listens to foreign radio stations, 29% listen to national news and 12% listen to local radio news stations. Only 33% believe they

get an accurate picture of the political life in their country and 57% were convinced that they could not rely on domestic political news. (RFE/RL)

Furat Valeev, editor-in-chief of the daily *Vetchernij Neftekamsk* in the republic of Bashkortostan, was sentenced to ten days' imprisonment in Neftekamsk Prison on 4 October for 'disrespecting the court'. Valeev published an article in May drawing attention to corruption. Furthermore, he had never received the court notice that action had been taken against him. Two military officers came to the daily's offices and took him to court. (GDF)

A novel by the Voronezh writer **Nadezhda Seredina**, which had 2,000 copies printed and had been reviewed in Voronezh newspapers, has not been released. The novel is set in the early 1990s and incorporates documentary material. A letter from the Voronezh Regional Cultural Committee claimed that due to 'irregularities' in the original contract, the publishers Modek are under no legal obligation to proceed with publication. (*Index*)

SERBIA

Former president and mentor of Slobodan Milosevic, **Ivan Stambolic**, went missing on 15 August. On 30 August the regime daily *Politika*, and on 31 August the daily *Politika Ekspres*, published articles exposing Stambolic's alleged dealings with companies from Republika Srpska and Montenegro, stating these would provide the motive. On 8 September, his wife **Katarina**

Credit: Focus Communication

On Friday 6 September, a group of Otpor activists liberated the premises of Radio B92 and handed the station back to its real owners. None of the station's owners had been inside the premises since 2 April 1999 when, after an illegal decision by the Belgrade Business Court, the director of Radio B92 was dismissed by a new pro-regime management and employees were denied access (*Index* 3/1999). This was the third banning of Belgrade's highest-rated independent radio station. All permanent staff were sacked by the usurping management, and associate contributors left in solidarity. They stayed together to launch Free B92 and, in August 1999, resumed broadcasting as Radio B2-92 on the third frequency of Studio B Radio until that station was taken over by the government on 17 May of this year (*Index* 3/2000).

After the takeover of Studio B, Radio B2-92 re-emerged as a regional radio and television station in collaboration with all stations on the ANEM network and other friendly electronic media in the region. News was distributed 24 hours a day on a radio programme transmitting on several frequencies in an attempt to avoid signal jamming. It was also broadcast on Net radio on the most frequently visited website in Yugoslavia.

With the return to the premises of the original Radio B92 in the Dom Omladine building in central Belgrade, the wheel has turned full circle. (ANEM)

Stambolic, a lawyer, and the daily *Danas* received anonymous phone calls informing them that Stambolic had been seen being removed from Belgrade's main prison a week earlier. (Free Serbia)

Journalist **Zoran Lukovic**, with the independent daily *Dveni Telegraf*, was arrested and transferred to prison on 15 August when he went to a Belgrade police station to extend his registration papers (*Index* 3/1999. (ANEM)

From 18 August onwards, the signal of independent Nis NTV in Leskovac was severely disrupted, particularly during news broadcasts. (ANEM)

Fourteen Otpor activists were arrested in Sombor on 23 August. The acting director of *Somborske novine* **Danilo Sekulic** and Radio Sombor journalist **Stipan Benic** were released at 5pm, but the acting director of Radio Sombor, **Anita Beretic**, was detained after refusing to remove the Otpor T-shirt she was wearing. (ANEM)

On 25 August director **Natasa Kandic** of the Humanitarian Law Centre was threatened with criminal charges by the army for making allegations of government atrocities in an article in *Danas*. Kandic maintains that her comments were based on witness statements. (ANEM, HRW, GHM)

On 27 August, the Montenegrin authorities banned state media from broadcasting or publishing any of the federal election campaign on the grounds that the election was illegal. (ANEM)

Photographer **Mara Babovic** and the crew of Podgorica daily *Pobjeda* were arrested by the army on 28 August while trying to get permission to photograph military barricades in the Pljevlje settlement of Sule during a rally. (ANEM)

Research commissioned by the Media Centre showed that, in the last week of August, Radio Television Serbia devoted nine hours and 38 minutes in prime-time news programmes to the Socialists and Yugoslav Left members. The Democratic Opposition enjoyed 21 minutes of programming, all of which was negative. The winning candidate, Vojislav Kostunica, was mentioned only once. (ANEM)

TV Rosulja, the only station in the Jablanica district to offer paid slots on air to opposition parties, was evicted on 7 September. (ANEM)

Journalist with the Serbian programme of Kosovo Radio-TV and multi-ethnic Pristina station Radio Kontakt, **Marjan Melonasi**, went missing in Pristina on 9 September. His colleagues attribute his abduction to the fact that he spoke Serbian in public, something that very few Albanians in Kosovo do. (IPI, ANEM)

TV Cacak, municipal station for Gornji Milanovac, lost its signal on 9 September for reporting the Kostunica election campaign. (RSF, GHM)

Shefki Popova, an Albanian Kosovar journalist who worked for the daily *Rilindja* for 26 years, was shot, stabbed and killed on

10 September near the cultural centre of Vucitrn, near Pristina. He died on the way to hospital. (RSF, IFJ, IPI)

Having had a 12-year jail conviction overturned in June by the Supreme Court, the poet, paediatrician and women's rights activist **Flora Brovina** had new proceedings brought against her on 14 September at Nis District Court. (PEN)

Radio Jasenica in Smedereska Palank experienced such disruption to its signal on 19 September that management filed a complaint with the police. The transmitter for Television Pirot in Dimitrovgrad was cut off on 19 September, apparently by the local electricity company. A screen ticker informing the citizens of Pozorevac of the call for a general strike was interrupted on 20 September. The frequency of Radio 021 from Novi Sad was jammed on 21 September. Twenty foreign reporters were given 24 hours to leave on 22 September without explanation. The video beam that was to broadcast the election results in Leskovac was confiscated on 24 September by police while being transported from Kragujevac. Belgrade-based Radio Index was forced to stop broadcasting on 25 September between 7.30 and 8pm when a shrill noise disrupted its frequency. (ANEM, Free Media, RSF, IFJ, IPI)

SIERRA LEONE

Mustapha Bai Attilla, a blind reporter from the radio station Voice of the Handicapped, was on 7 October forcefully separated from his two guides and,

Talk Radio 702

JOHN ROBBIE: **Do you accept that HIV causes AIDS?**

HEALTH MINISTER MANTO TSHABALALA-MSIMANG: I have answered that question umpteen times.

Yes, and the answer is?

Umpteen times I have answered that question. My whole track record of having worked in the area of HIV for the last 20 years is testimony.

You haven't answered the question, Manto.

Why should you ask me that question?

To avoid confusion.

I have never said anything contrary to what you want me to say today.

So, therefore, you accept that HIV causes AIDS?

You are not going to put words into my mouth.

I am not putting words into your mouth. I am asking you a question.

Yes you are.

I am asking you a straight question, the minister of health of South Africa, I am asking you: does HIV cause AIDS?

I have been party to developing a strategic framework and that strategy testifies what my policy understandings of the HIV epidemic are. If you haven't read that, please go and read it …

Manto, Manto. A simple yes or no is the answer I am looking for.

You will not force me into a corner into saying yes or no.

I find your reaction bizarre.

I would advise you to read the strategic framework. It is important for the media to inform the public about the positions of government. It is time that, when you interview people – not on 'yes' or 'no', but on the tenets of the framework.

Manto, we have gone as far as we can go.

I am not Manto to you. Let me tell you I am not Manto to you.

How must I address you?

I don't know – but you have to read the strategic framework.

Bizarre.

And I …

Oh go away!

And I am …

I cannot take that rubbish any longer. Can you believe it? I have never in my life heard such rubbish. ❏

On 14 September the ANC called on radio station Talk Radio 702 to dismiss presenter **John Robbie** *after he clashed with Health Minister Manto Tshabalala-Msimang on air when she refused to say whether she believed HIV caused AIDS (*Index 5/2000*).*

amid shouts to 'keep his mouth shut', beaten up by officials of the ministry of transport and communications. On several occasions Attilla had exposed corruption at the state-owned company Sierratel. (RSF)

SOLOMON ISLANDS

Freelance journalist **Duran Angiki**, who has been covering the separatist crisis for independent news websites, is reported to have received several threatening phone calls at home on 27 and 28 September over an article published by the Pasifik Nius website concerning payments made to the leader of the Malaita Eagle Force, Andrew Nori. (Pacific Media Watch)

SOUTH AFRICA

Freelance journalist **Dale T McKinley** has been expelled by the South African Communist Party (SACP) for publicly attacking and questioning the bona fides and integrity of the party, its leaders and two of its union allies, it was reported on 11 August. It appears that the material of the contested articles which he wrote for both local and international outlets was contained in a book McKinley published in 1997. His problems with the SACP seem to have arisen earlier this year when he decided to go freelance. (Free Expression Institute)

The Human Rights Commission report of its investigation into 'subliminal racism' in the country's media, published in late August, found that, while the media could be characterised

as racist institutions, there was no evidence of them indulging in the 'blatant advocacy of racial hatred or incitement to racial violence' (*Index* 2/2000, 3/2000). (Free Expression Institute)

After President Thabo Mbeki aired his controversial views on the origins of HIV in an interview with *Time* magazine in September (*Index* 5/2000), the *Sunday Independent*, owned by Tony O'Reilly's Argus Newspapers, offered free advertising space to defend his opinions. On 11 October, the paper's unnamed editor wrote in an editorial: 'This newspaper wants to state categorically that it is against its policy to offer the government – or any other body – free space when the content is of a contentious political nature.' (*Private Eye*)

SPAIN

Six people were injured after a bomb exploded on 29 September in the Barcelona offices of the daily *El Mundo*. Three masked individuals, two men and a woman, overpowered security guards, entered the building and deposited a parcel containing explosives in a wastepaper bin. Before fleeing, they identified themselves as members of the October Anti-Fascist Resistance Group. The building was evacuated prior to the blast which severely damaged the newspaper's offices. (Associated Press, *Guardian*)

Anti-terrorism police exploded a package addressed to **Alfredo Semprun**, assistant director at the Madrid branch of the newspaper *La Razon*. The book-like parcel had the sender as the

Barcelona office of the newspaper. Police sources attribute the attempt to a group called The Anarchists, who campaign for the rights of the prisoners under special guard. This group has sent a dozen such packages to journalists. (*El Pais*)

SRI LANKA

Sinhala-language newspapers *Lankadipa* and *Divaina*, and the English-language *Daily Mirror*, *Island* and *Sunday Leader* all received warnings from Director of Information Ariya Rubasinghe in the last two weeks of August. In a statement to the media, Rubasinghe complained about news items that 'create dissension among the security forces' by alluding to problems within the army. Demoralising the security forces is illegal under Emergency Regulations promulgated in 1 July. (CPJ)

Lasantha Wickrematunga, editor of the English-language *Sunday Leader*, was sentenced to two years' imprisonment on 5 September suspended for five years, for defaming President Chandrika Kumaratunga. If convicted of any other sentence during the next five years, Wickrematunga will have to serve his term. The charge was based on an article he wrote criticising the president for failing to carry out election promises. (CPJ, IPI)

On 5 September, the government temporarily suspended emergency regulations 12 (1) and 14, banning public meetings and giving the administration broad censoring powers, respectively. (CPJ, BBC)

●●●●●●●●●●●●●●●●●●●●●●●●●●●●●●●●●●●

Martial arts

Abdelhadi Abbas (lawyer and writer), Abdelmu'in Mlouhi (member of the
Arabic Language Academy), Antoine Makdessi (writer and thinker), Burhan
Ghalyoun (writer and thinker), Sadek Jalal al-Azm (writer and thinker), Michael
Kilo (writer), Tayyeb Tayzini (writer and thinker), Abderrahman Munif
(novelist), Adonis (poet), Burhan Bukhari (researcher), Hanna Abboud (writer),
Omar Amiralay (cinematographer), Khaled Taja (actor), Bassam Koussa (actor),
Ms Nayla al-Atrash (theatre producer), Abdullah Hanna (researcher and
historian), Samir Suaifin (economist), Faisal Darraj (researcher), Haidar Haidar
(novelist), Nazih Abu-'Afsh (poet), Hassan M Youssef (journalist and author),
Usama Mohammad (cinematographer), Nabil Suleiman (novelist and critic),
Abderrazzak Eid (researcher and critic), Jad al-Karim Jaba'i (writer and
researcher), Abdellatif Abdelhamid (cinematographer), Samir Zekra (cinematographer), Ahmad Mu'alla (impressionist), Faris Helou (actor), Ihsan Abbas
(researcher), Ms Hanan Kassab-Hassan (professor), Mamdouh Azzam (novelist),
Adel Mahmoud (poet), Hazem al-Azmeh (physician and professor), Burhan
Zraik (lawyer), Mohammad Ra'doun (lawyer), Yasser Sari (lawyer), Youssef
Salman (translator), Ms Hind Midani (cinematographer), Munzer Masri (poet
and impressionist), Ahmad Mu'aita (professor), Wafik Slaitin (professor), Majab
al-Imam (professor), Munzer Halloum (professor), Malek Suleiman (professor),
Ms Sarab Jamal al-Atassi (researcher), Tewfik Haroun (lawyer), Issam Suleiman
(physician), Joseph Lahham (lawyer), Atiyych Massouh (researcher), Radwan
Kadmani (professor), Nizar Sabour (impressionist), Shuaib Tlaimat (professor),
Hassan Sami Youssef (cinematographer and writer), Ms Waha al-Raheb
(actress), Hamid Mer'i (economist), Rif'at Sioufi (engineer), Mouwaffak
Nirbiya (writer), Suhail Shbat (professor), Jamal Shuhaid (professor), Omar
Kosh (writer), Raymond Boutros (cinemaographer), Ms Antoinette Azriyeh
(cinemaographer), Najeeb Nsair (critic and writer), Ms May Skaff (actress),
Nidal Debs (cinematographer), Ms Farah Joukhdar (architect), Akram Katrceb
(poet), Lukman Dabraki (poet), Hikmat Shatta (architect), Mohammad Najati
Tayyara (researcher), Nejmeddin as-Samman (author), Ali al-Saleh (economist)
Ms Sabah al-Hallak (researcher), and others. ❏

*On 27 September 99 Syrian writers, artists and intellectuals issued a statement in
a Lebanese newspaper calling for the lifting of martial law and the release of political
prisoners. They urged that public life be freed from the 'laws, restraints and various forms
of censorship imposed on it, such that citizens would be allowed to give expression to their
various interests within the framework of a social concord'.*

●●●●●●●●●●●●●●●●●●●●●●●●●●●●●●●●●●●

SUDAN

Journalist **Osmane Mirghani** with the private daily *Al Rai al A'am* was arrested in connection with an article on 24 August in which he called the justice ministry a 'scarecrow' in its handling of corruption cases. The journalist has repeatedly been detained over articles on financial corruption and social disintegration. On 25 August, journalist **Alula Berhe Kedani** with *Al Rai Al Akhar* was arrested by security services. The reason for his arrest has not been explained. (RSF)

Mohamed Taha Mohamed Ahmed, editor-in-chief of the daily *Al Wifaq*, survived an apparent murder attempt on 26 September when he was knocked down by a car as he left the offices of the National Press Council. He had earlier given evidence to the Council of the National Congress of the People over an article allegedly defamatory of Hassan El Tourabi, the president of the National Press Council and *éminence grise* of the military government until his recent fall from grace. *Al Wifaq* was ordered to close for five days. (CJFE)

SYRIA

New ground was broken on 2 October when the official newspaper *Al-Thawra* published a two-page article by **Professor Arif Dalila**, a prominent member of the emerging civil rights movement, denouncing state-management of the economy. The article was considered 'an unprecedented critique in a hitherto sterile Syrian press'. (BBC)

TAJIKISTAN

On 27 August **Nematulloi Nurullo**, a reporter with the newspaper *Dzhumkhuriyat*, was forced into a car and taken to a police station. He was so severely beaten he suffered concussion and loss of hearing in one ear. (CJES)

TANZANIA

The government has banned a gospel cassette by evangelist **Faustin Munishi**, a Tanzanian based in Kenya. On 22 September, Munishi said that he had been forced to leave Tanzania and that his life was now in danger. (NDIMA)

TUNISIA

On 25 September two French journalists were harassed by police while covering the return to Tunis of exiled writer **Taoufik Ben Brik** (*Index* 4/1999, 2/2000, 4/2000). **Daniel Mermet** and **Giv Anquetil**, both reporters for France Inter, were prevented from boarding a Paris-bound flight by airport officials, who demanded that they hand over interview cassettes. The two men, however, duped the security officers by concealing the recordings in their luggage and giving the authorities blank tapes instead. (Agence France-Presse)

TURKMENISTAN

RFE/RL Turkman reporter **Saparurat Ovezberdiev** was told by the authorities on 17 August he must stop reporting because he does not have the accreditations to engage in journalism. Despite political pressure, however, he will continue to report since RFE/RL has official permission from the foreign ministry. (RFE/RL)

TURKEY

The Istanbul State Security Court confiscated the 2 August issue of *Milli Gazete* (National Gazette) and the latest issue of the journal *Partizan* for articles violating laws on propaganda and civil service practice. (*Evrensel*, *Yeni Safak*)

A cameraman for Flash TV, **Unal Cetiner**, was injured by police and his camera damaged during a demonstration in Istanbul against a new type of isolation cell in prisons. (RSF)

A trial is to be launched against Human Rights Association chairwoman **Eren Keskin** for 'insulting the military' in her interview published in the journal, *Cuma*, a pro-Islamic publication. Keskin faces a possible jail term of up to six years, along with *Cuma* editor-in-chief **Mehmet Ozen** and reporter **Ramazan Gozubuyuk**. (*Yeni Gundem*)

On 5 August **Karip Polat**, owner of *Turkman* and *Asi* magazines; **Dogan Tolu**, managing editor of *Turkman*, and an employee, **Ferdane Tolu**; **Gulay Arslan**, editor of *Asi*, and employees **Suleyman Ozalp**, **Gultekin Arslan** and **Sunay Demir** were interrogated by police in Burnaz, southern Turkey. On 9 August Sunay Demir and Ferdane Tolu were released, but the others have been imprisoned for alleged membership of an illegal organisation. (RSF)

Mikhail Vayic, owner and editor-in-chief of the weekly *Yasamda Atilim*, was arrested by military officers on 14 August after visiting a relative in Gebze prison (near Istanbul). He was imprisoned the following day for 'possession of illegal magazines'. (RSF)

Reporter **Julide Kalic**, of the daily *Yeni Evrensel*, was beaten and interrogated after photographing a police attack on a remembrance day meeting for Haci Bektas-i Veli, a 13th-century scholar who has a cult following. She was driven to a far-off police station and her film confiscated. (RSF)

Officials have put pressure on the management of Microsoft to modify an article in its digital encyclopaedia, *Encarta*, that calls the murder of thousands of Armenians by the Ottoman Empire 'the first genocide of the 20th century'. The authors were asked to 'tone down' the article and remove the word 'genocide'. One of the writers, **Ronald Grigor Suny**, said the editors had indicated that there had been some threats from the government to arrest Microsoft officials in Turkey and even ban Microsoft products. Microsoft has denied receiving such threats and Ankara denies making them. (CNN)

A reporter with bi-monthly *Devrimci Demokrasi*, **Tuncay Sezgin**, was beaten and threatened by police in a courthouse. He was covering the trial of some demonstrators protesting against a new type of prison on 21 August. (RSF)

Editor-in-chief of the daily *Evrensel* (*Index* 3/1996, 4/1996, 4/2000) **Fatih Polat**, and responsible editor-in-chief **Bulent Falakoglu** went on trial in August charged with 'insulting the army' in articles published in several editions of the paper this year. *Yeni Evrensel* was ordered to close for ten days on 6 October for publishing an article by **A Cihan Soylu**, 'Kurdish Problem or The Struggle for Full Equality of Rights'. (Campaign For Human Rights in Turkey, RSF)

Malatya-based Gunes TV and Er TV were both closed down for seven days on 15 August for broadcasting news reports of police attacks on prisoners. Since 1 January this year, the Supreme Board of Radio and Television has handed out 3,761 days worth of suspensions to 25 radio stations and 27 television stations. (*Yeni Gundem*, Kurdistan Observer, RSF)

Police detained **Kemal Acar** and **Idris Yilmaz**, Adana distributors for the daily *Yeni Gundem*, on 26 August. They were taken to a local police station, beaten up and told to stop distributing the daily. On 30 August five people were detained when police raided the Ankara office of the journal, *Vatan*. (*Yeni Gundem*, *Cumhuriyet*)

Three journalists with Kurdish daily *Yeni Gundem*, **Erguren Top**, **Cengiz Kapmaz** and **Meral Kocamis**, were detained by police for covering the press conference held by relatives of political prisoners. Erguren Top had to be taken to hospital for

treatment, but all three were released after the intervention of the newspaper's director and lawyer. (RSF)

On 31 August the Kurdish daily *Yeni Gundem* was seized by the Security Court of the State of Istanbul. The newspaper was accused of 'separatist propaganda' for having published an article entitled 'The Kurdish revolution'. (RSF)

Mehmet Ali Birand (*Index* 3/1998, 4/1998, 3/2000), a prominent journalist and presenter for TV station CNN-Turk, has been charged with aiding an outlawed group, the Great Eastern Islamic Raiders' Front (IBDA-C), by allowing the group to 'air its propaganda'. Birand conducted a live telephone interview with prisoner **Burak Cileli** in January, while Cileli and other IBDA-C inmates held 17 guards and a lawyer hostage for six hours. Birand faces up to three years and nine months in prison if convicted. (Associated Press, Kurdish Media)

Nadire Mater (*Index* 5/1999, 6/1999), the woman journalist on trial for 'insulting' the military in a book of interviews with former conscripts of the war in the south-east, was acquitted of all charges on 29 September. Mater, who writes for the news agency Inter Press Service, had been on trial since June last year after the fifth edition of *Mehmet's Book* was banned from distribution and confiscated from booksellers. Mater's publisher, **Samih Sokman**, who had faced a potentially large fine, was also acquitted. (CPJ, Amnesty)

Former president of the Human Rights Association (IHD), **Akin Birdal**, (*Index* 4/1998, 5/1998, 1/1999, 4/1999, 6/1999, 1/2000, 2/2000, 3/2000) was released from prison on 23 September. Birdal had served ten months for 'provoking racial hatred' by his calls for a peaceful solution to the Kurdish conflict in 1995 and 1996. On his release he declared: 'I hope I will be the last victim of any "thought crimes". While my democratic and political rights were suspended under Article 312, I will continue to work for democracy and peace.' (*Cildekt*)

Suat Özalp, Diyarbakir regional representative of the weekly *Azadiya Welat*, who was detained in Diyarbakir on 26 September, was released on 29 September. Özalp was reportedly warned not to work at the newspaper. (*Yeni Gundem*)

Six teachers were arrested in the regional capital of Diyarbakir on 4 October for sending out invitations to a World Teachers Day celebration, written in both Turkish and Kurdish. The police claimed that 'publishing and distributing invitations in Kurdish is a crime under the law'. (Kurdistan Observer)

Officials warned the US that it risked losing the use of a military base for launching air patrols over northern Iraq if the House of Representatives approved a resolution accusing Turkey of genocide against Armenians 80 years ago. The resolution is a symbolic measure for focusing on the forced eviction and murder of as many as 1.5 million Armenians between 1915 and 1923. Turkey has refused to acknowl-

edge the massacres that led to the near-annihilation of the Armenians in Ottoman Turkey. (*Washington Post*)

Two books have been confiscated after just ten hours of being on sale. **Mahmut Baksi**'s *Rome Marches* (*Index* 4/2000, 5/2000) and a 334-page compilation of former PKK president Abdullah Ocalan's talks, entitled *Talks from Rome*, were published by Aram Publishing House on 5 September. The next day the Istanbul State security Court banned them and all copies were confiscated. **Abdullah Gunduz**, of Aram Publishing, commented that 21 of the 24 books the company has published have been confiscated so far. (Kurdish Observer)

UKRAINE

After complaining of harassment by the police, **Georgy Gongadze**, editor of the Internet newsletter *Pravade Ukrayiny*, failed to return to his home in Kiev on 16 September after leaving a colleague's house around 10.20 that evening. The newsletter often features articles critical of government officials with reports of alleged corruption. Police have ruled out any political motives, suggesting his disappearance was connected to his personal life. The site had often published material from the 'Agency of Federal Investigations', a media outlet that has received threats for its commentary on government officials. **Oleh Yeltsov**, a reporter with *Pravade Ukrayiny*, received threats following the publication of an article on Oleksandr Volkov, leader of Vidrodzehenya Rehioniv

(Regional Rebirth) parliamentary group. It is unclear whether the threats were a direct result of this or other articles. (CPJ, IPI)

In the city of Cherkassy, freelance journalist **Valentina Vasilchenkp** was assaulted on the stairwell of her apartment building on 14 August for a series of articles on police corruption published in the independent weekly *Antenna*. (IPI)

USA

Newly declassified governments documents show that in the 1950s and 1960s US intelligence funded and directed a campaign to bring about a federal Europe, it was reported on 19 September. One memorandum, dated 26 July 1950 and among documents found by Georgetown University researcher Joshua Paul, gives instructions for a campaign to promote an all-powerful European parliament and is signed by General William J Donovan, head of the organisation which became the CIA. The European Movement, the most important pro-Europe organisation of the post-war years, was largely funded by the US and efforts by members to raise money in Europe were reprimanded by American paymasters. The former vice-president of the European Economic Community, Robert Marjolin, was advised, while in office in 1965, to try to achieve monetary union by 'stealth' in a memo which recommends the restriction of debate on the subject until such time as 'the adoption of such proposals would become virtually inescapable'. (*Daily Telegraph*)

A Florida court found that Rupert Murdoch's Fox TV had acted intentionally and deliberately to falsify or distort two journalists' news reporting and awarded them US$425,000 in damages, it was reported on 8 September. **Steve Wilson** and **Jane Akre** were fired by Fox TV after they threatened to blow the whistle on the distortion of their 1997 report on the use of potentially carcinogenic hormones on cows by milk producers in Florida (*Index* 3/2000). Wilson and Akre refused to report the distorted version which had been created after the manufacturer of the hormones, Monsanto, asked for 70 rewrites of the original script. (*BGHBulletin*)

The civilian editor of a government newspaper aimed at US troops abroad resigned as a result of pressure from the Pentagon to kill a story, it was reported on 1 September. **David Offer**, 58, resigned from his post at *Stars and Stripes* after he was told that a story he was planning to run, concerning the placing on alert of US units in Germany due to concern that Iraq might attack Israel, contained classified information and should not be made public. The *Washington Post* subsequently ran the story, but Offer was still not allowed to publish it in his paper. 'It's absurd and it's unacceptable. This is news management by the military,' he said. (CNN.com)

URUGUAY

La Marea FM, a community radio station in the rural village of Barra de Valijas, has been forced off the air following a raid by judicial authorities on 1 September. Police and army personnel seized the station's transmitter, antenna and other equipment. The judge who ordered the raid said that La Marea FM's signal was interfering with broadcasts from the ministry of national defence. (AMARC)

ZAMBIA

On 25 August **Henry Chilufya**, deputy news editor of the privately owned Radio Phoenix, was illegally detained and harassed for at least an hour by members of the ruling Movement for Multi-Party Democracy (MMD) in Lusaka. Chilufya was on an assignment investigating reports of MMD involvement in extortion when he was assaulted. (MISA)

ZIMBABWE

On 18 August the government asked the eight-member board of state-owned Zimpapers to resign. It is believed that the changes are part of a plan by the new Minister of Information and Publicity, Jonathan Moyo, to further tighten state control of news content. (MISA)

Standard journalist **Chengetai Zvauya** has been repeatedly threatened by former chairperson of the Zimbabwe War Veterans Association, Chenjeai Hunzvie, for allegedly writing critical stories about him. Zvauya was harassed and thrown out of a Hunzvie news conference despite being invited to the conference by the War Veterans Association (*Index* 5/2000). (MISA)

A Supreme Court ruling on 22 September has nullified Sections 27 and 28 of the Broadcasting Act which protects the Zimbabwe Broadcasting Corporation's monopoly on broadcasting. The government responded by saying it would comply with the ruling and would start drawing up regulatory mechanisms. (Media Monitoring Project)

On 5 October police forced their way into the studios of the country's first independent station, Capital Radio, halting transmission and seizing the station's electronic equipment. Capital began broadcasting at the end of September following the High Court ruling that ended the government's monopoly. However, on 4 October President Robert Mugabe overruled the court and signed an order outlawing private broadcasting without state approval. As a result of the raid, station director **Michael Auret** and presenter **Gerry Jackson** were forced into hiding. (MISA, *Daily Telegraph*)

Compiled by: Andrew Barsoum, Gbenga Oduntan, Shifa Rahman (Africa); Ben Carrdus, Louise Finer, Anna Lloyd, Jessica Smith-Rohrberg (Asia); William Escofet, Mebrak Tareke (South and Central America); David Gelber, Gill Newsham, Neil Sammonds (Middle East); Humfrey Hunter (North America and Pacific); Louise Finer, Deborah Haynes (UK and western Europe); Louise Finer, Katy Sheppard (eastern Europe and the Balkans).

Support for

INDEX
ON CENSORSHIP

It is the generosity of our friends and supporters that makes *Index on Censorship*'s work possible. *Index* remains the only international publication devoted to the promotion and protection of that basic, yet still abused, human right – freedom of expression.

Your support is needed more than ever now as *Index* and the Writers and Scholars Educational Trust continue to grow and develop new projects. Donations will enable us to expand our website, which will make access to *Index*'s stories and communication between free speech activists and supporters even easier, and will help directly in our education programme. This will see *Index*, for the first time, fostering a better understanding of censorship and anti-censorship issues in schools.

Please help *Index* speak out.

The Trustees and Directors would like to thank the many individuals and organisations who support *Index on Censorship* and the Writers and Scholars Educational Trust, including:

If you would like more information about *Index on Censorship* or would like to support our work, please contact Hugo Grieve, Fundraising Manager, on (44) 20 7278 2313 or email hugo@indexoncensorship.org